MICROWAVE AND FREEZER COOKERY

MICROWAVE AND FREEZER COOKERY

Carol Bowen

CONTENTS

First published in 1985 by Octopus Books Limited
59 Grosvenor Street, London W1

Third impression, 1986

© 1985 Hennerwood Publications Limited

ISBN 0 86273 230 1

Printed in Hong Kong

INTRODUCTION

It is hardly surprising that the microwave cooker has often been called, justifiably, the 'unfreezer' – for its ability to thaw and cook or reheat foods in minutes rather than hours is quite remarkable. It is this unique and special friendship between microwave and freezer that attracts it to, and makes it popular with, so many different cooks: the housewife who economically batch-cooks family meals; the busy 'career' cook who has little time to sort out and select frozen food in the morning for an evening meal; the cook-ahead hostess who derives comfort from knowing there is always a meal-on-ice; and the 'instant-eater' cook – child, teenager or adult who enjoys a frozen snack out of usual mealtime hours at short notice.

In recognition of this special and useful action, most microwave cookers have a defrost power facility on their control dial. Thawing takes place in these by giving the food a short burst of microwave energy, followed by a rest period, and then repeating the process until the food is evenly thawed.

MICROWAVE COOKING INSTRUCTIONS

Just as we observe certain procedures in conventional cooking, it is also important to follow a few guidelines in using a microwave. Whether you are cooking from fresh, frozen or thawed state, it is important to turn, stir, rotate and re-arrange foods to ensure they defrost or cook evenly.

Turning food over is common in conventional cooking and is equally necessary in microwave cooking. In most cases, turn the food over, where possible, halfway through the cooking time, unless the recipe specifies more regular turning. This is not generally done in isolation, but in combination with either stirring, rotating or re-arranging foods.

Microwaves only penetrate foods to a certain depth so **stirring** is necessary to distribute heat evenly. A wooden spoon or spatula will help you stir foods from the outside of the dish (where they receive most energy and therefore cook faster) to the inside (where they receive least energy and therefore cook more slowly).

When a food cannot be stirred or turned over, it is important to **rotate** the food or dish. In most cases a quarter or half-turn halfway through the cooking time is all that is needed. The recipes in this book assume that your microwave cooker does not have a turntable. If it does have one, refer to the manufacturer's instructions.

Another way of ensuring that a food cooks evenly is to **re-arrange** it during cooking. You will probably find that your oven has hot and cold spots since no microwave has a perfectly tuned energy distribution pattern. Re-arranging foods halfway

through the cooking time overcomes such energy 'blackspots'.

Covering food is often necessary in microwave cooking. It can speed up cooking time, prevent drying out or reduce spattering of cooking juices on to the sides of the oven. There are several effective ways of covering: use a tight-fitting lid to a dish or cover a lidless dish with a saucer or plate; place food in a roaster or cook-in bag but replace the metal ties with string or elastic bands; cover fatty foods like bacon, or set moisture-laden foods like jacket potatoes on a paper towel; mould a tight 'lid' of cling film over a dish but pierce in a couple of places to prevent a 'ballooning' effect; or cover an irregular-shaped food with greaseproof paper and secure around the dish with string or tuck under the base.

Remember too that with the speed of microwave cooking pressure mounts quickly from the production of steam, so prick or pierce cook-in bags, cling film, boil-in-bag pouches, egg yolks, sausages, jacket potatoes and any other foods with a tight-fitting membrane, to **release pressure**.

It is less critical but useful to **remove excess juices** during cooking because these attract microwave energy and in effect slow down the cooking process. It is best to use a bulb baster for this (a kind of syringe consisting of a plastic tube with a rubber bulb at one end, available from hardware or cookery shops). If a food starts to dry out towards the end of cooking, the juices can always be re-introduced.

Shielding is a technique employed to protect vulnerable parts of a food from overcooking. These include the wing tips, drumsticks and tail-end of poultry and game birds, the heads and tails of fish, the thinner end of lamb or pork, and any fatty areas, like the rind of a piece of pork or ham. **Small strips of aluminium foil are used to cover the sensitive parts – this is the only time when small pieces of metal may be introduced into the microwave oven cavity. Either add the aluminium foil before cooking and remove halfway through the cooking time, or add to the areas as they seem to be just cooked. Ensure that the aluminium foil never touches the sides of the oven. Make certain that the area uncovered is much greater than the area covered with foil or the microwaves may 'arc'. If a dish sparks due to arcing the oven should be switched off immediately and any metal removed before cooking recommences. Also check with the manufacturer's instructions.**

Cooking continues after the microwave energy has been turned off. This is due to the conduction of heat within the food. This can clearly be seen when baking cakes – when cooked sufficiently, most cakes will still appear wet and tacky on the surface, but while standing the crust will dry out and cook with the conducted heat in the cake. It is therefore important to **observe standing times** when cooking and thawing food.

Foods that need to be served hot are best covered with aluminium foil while standing. The foil serves to trap the heat in the food, keeping it hot enough to serve without reheating.

Just as we arrange food carefully in a conventional oven, we must **arrange food correctly** to make the most of microwave energy. Several items of the same food should be arranged in a ring pattern for even cooking, for the centre of a dish receives less microwave energy while the sides receive equal amounts. Unevenly-shaped foods like chicken drumsticks and broccoli should therefore be placed with the thinner parts to the centre.

DISHES AND UTENSILS

Refer to the manufacturer's instructions for which dishes and utensils are suitable. If you are planning to cook and freeze in the same container, check that it is suitable for both processes. Some manufacturers have introduced special freezer-to-microwave cookware, which can be used for prime cooking, thawing and reheating. Some dishes double up for use in the conventional oven – but not above temperatures of 200°C (400°F) and certainly not under a grill.

If a cooking dish does not seem suitable for freezing, transfer the food to a rigid freezer-proof container for freezing and return to a serving dish for defrosting and reheating.

If you are using freezer bags, replace the metal ties with string or elastic bands, and remember to remove any metal caps or lids from convenience style frozen foods before defrosting or reheating. Remember also to allow headspace when freezing liquids.

Shapes of dishes are also important. Round and ring shapes give best results and shallow dishes also prove better than deep ones. Square, oval and rectangular shapes are less efficient since the energy seems to concentrate in the corners – although you can shield corners with small strips of aluminium foil (page 6) to prevent overcooking. Finally, try to use a straight-sided dish which will allow the microwaves to penetrate more evenly, giving good cooking or reheating results.

SPECIAL COOKING TECHNIQUES

Some foods, fresh or frozen, require special attention during microwave cooking for perfect results:

Fish and shellfish
- Shield the head and tail of whole fish with aluminium foil (page 6) during thawing and cooking. Cut the skin in 2 or 3 places to prevent bursting during cooking.
- Arrange fish fillets so that the thinner tails are to the centre of the dish.
- Arrange peeled shellfish in a ring pattern in a dish. Break up a frozen block of shellfish 2 or 3 times during thawing.

Poultry and game
- Shield the wing tips, drumsticks and tail-end of birds with aluminium foil (page 6) during thawing and cooking.
- Arrange poultry pieces for thawing and cooking with the meatiest portions to the outside of the dish.
- Prick giblets and livers before cooking to prevent bursting.

Meat
- Break up minced beef, pork or lamb once or twice during thawing and cooking.
- Shield thin ends of roasts with aluminium foil (page 6) during thawing and cooking.
- Ideally, bone and roll meat into a neat shape for cooking.
- Prick sausages, liver and kidneys before thawing and cooking.
- Arrange the thinner ends of chops to centre of a dish for thawing and cooking.

Vegetables
- Ideally, trim vegetables to a uniform size for cooking.
- Large or uneven vegetable pieces should be arranged with the thinner part to the centre of the dish.
- Pierce any vegetables that have tight skins like potatoes, aubergines or marrow before cooking. Pierce boil-in-bag vegetables before defrosting and cooking.

Eggs and cheese
- Prick egg yolks with the tip of a knife or cocktail stick before cooking.
- Never attempt to cook an egg in its shell – it will explode.
- The fats in cheese attract microwave energy, so undercook rather than overcook initially to prevent stringiness.

Fruit
- Pierce fruits in tight skins like apples and pears before cooking.

Puddings
- Cook baked fruits until barely fork tender, never fallen since they will continue to cook with the residual heat.
- Sponge and suet puddings will still have a sticky top when cooked – this will dry out upon standing.

Baking
- Grease dishes, line with cling film or line with greased greaseproof paper for cooking – never grease and flour or you will end up with an unpleasant looking and tasting film around the food.
- Never overcook – observe standing times meticulously.
- Turn and rotate dishes evenly for good results.

Preserves
- Use large cooking containers since mixtures bubble up high.
- Mixtures must reach a good rolling boil to ensure a good set – if in doubt add commercial pectin according to the manufacturer's instructions.

Drinks
- Remember to choose a large enough container – liquids quickly expand to the rim of the cup, mug or glass.
- Do not use lead crystal and mugs or cups with glued-on handles.
- Never attempt to thaw or heat drinks in narrow-necked bottles – pressure builds up in the lower part of the bottle, causing it to shatter.

A GUIDE TO THAWING
Precise thawing instructions have been given for all the recipes in this book. Always err on the side of safety and follow the minimum times, adding extra if the food is not sufficiently thawed. Special care should be taken with poultry. When completely thawed the wings and legs will be flexible and there will be no ice in the cavity. The following hints will also ensure good results:
- Pierce any skins, membranes or pouches before thawing.
- Turn foods over during thawing.
- If turning is not possible then rotate the dish during thawing.
- Flex any pouches that cannot be broken up or stirred during the thawing time and rotate frequently.
- Place any foods like cakes, bread rolls, sausage rolls and pastry items on a double sheet of paper towel during thawing to absorb any excess moisture.
- Any blocks of frozen food should be broken up with a fork during thawing so that the microwave energy can concentrate on the unfrozen block.
- Separate any blocks of frozen meats like hamburgers, sausages and steaks as they thaw.
- Remove any giblets from the cavity of chickens and other poultry or game birds as they thaw.
- Open all cartons and remove any lids and wrappings before thawing.
- Remove all thaw juices and drips from frozen foods during the defrosting time with a bulb baster (page 6).
- With items like meat joints, whole poultry and whole fish, thaw

the items until icy, then leave to thaw completely during the standing time.

- If any parts of the food start to thaw at too fast a rate or become warm, then shield or protect these areas with small strips of aluminium foil (page 6), attached with wooden cocktail sticks.
- Always observe a standing time action — foods will continue to thaw with the heat produced via conduction. Allow foods to thaw until just icy for best results.
- Home-frozen food tends to take longer to thaw than commercially frozen food because of the size of the ice crystals formed.
- When freezing a meal, do not overlap foods and place the thicker, denser items to the edges of the plate rather than the centre.

A GUIDE TO REHEATING

Most foods will reheat in the microwave cooker without loss of quality, flavour, colour and some nutrients. For best results follow the guidelines below:

- Arrange foods on a plate for reheating so that the thicker, denser and meatier portions are to the outer edge.
- Cover foods when reheating with a layer of cling film if there is no lid to retain moisture.
- When reheating observe the standing time action to make maximum use of the microwave energy and to prevent overcooking.
- When reheating potatoes in their jackets, breads, pastry items and other moist foods, place them on a sheet of paper towel so that it may absorb the moisture.
- Stir foods regularly while reheating. If stirring is not possible then rotate the food or dish or re-arrange it.

COOK'S PLAN

As a general rule for microwave cooking, cook the main course first. Most meat, poultry and fish dishes, especially those cooked in sauces, do improve upon standing and roasts are often easier to carve. If wrapped in aluminium foil during their standing time, they will often require no further reheating.

Obviously, cook foods that require a long standing time first. Last minute or quick-cooking dishes can be cooked during that standing time.

For ease of preparation and cooking, prepare starters and desserts well ahead and reheat if necessary just before serving. A pudding that needs little attention can often be cooked while you are eating the starter and main course.

Menu planning and serving food perfectly cooked is an art that comes with experience. Your microwave cooker will help you through this trial and error time if you err on the side of safety. Dishes that have become lukewarm will quickly reheat with perfect freshness rather than having a dried-out look. Certainly until you have got the measure of your microwave, do not attempt to reheat, thaw or even cook more than one dish in the oven at the same time — it is easy to overestimate the time required and forget the composition of the dish so that foods cook unevenly.

RECIPE GUIDELINES

It is most important to read the introductory section of this book before attempting recipes — the guidelines will arm you with a wealth of information for achieving good results.

The recipes that follow have been tested on a microwave oven with power rating of 650-700 watts without a turntable.

The recipes have been tested using three power levels: DEFROST, MEDIUM AND FULL. The chart below gives the approximate power input in watts at these levels (as well as LOW), and their relative cooking times. Consult your microwave handbook for similar power levels for guidance with this chart.

It is also important to remember that if your microwave has a power rating lower than 650-700 watts then longer cooking times will be required. The chart given below will give you guidelines as to how to adjust your cooking times — but a few trial and error cooking tests may be necessary.

GUIDE TO COMPARATIVE MICROWAVE OVEN CONTROL SETTINGS

SETTINGS USED IN THESE RECIPES	SETTINGS VARIATIONS ON POPULAR MICROWAVE OVENS				APPROXIMATE % POWER INPUT	APPROXIMATE POWER OUTPUT IN WATTS	COOKING TIMES (IN MINUTES) (for times greater than 10 minutes simply add together the figures in the appropriate columns)									
LOW	1	keep warm	low	2	25%	150W	4	8	12	16	20	24	28	32	36	40
	2	simmer		3	30%	200W	3¼	6¾	10	13¼	16¾	20	23¼	26¾	30	33¼
DEFROST	3	stew	medium/low	4	40%	250W	2½	5	7½	10	12½	15	17½	20	22½	25
MEDIUM	4	defrost	medium	5	50%	300W	2	4	6	8	10	12	14	16	18	20
	5	bake	medium	6	60%	400W	1¾	3¼	5	6¾	8¼	10	12	13¼	15	16½
	6	roast	high	7-8	75%	500-550W	1¼	2¾	4	5¼	6¾	8	9¼	10¾	12	13¼
FULL/ MAXIMUM	7	full/high	normal	10	100%	650-700W	1	2	3	4	5	6	7	8	9	10

SUPPERS AND SNACKS

SAUSAGE RISOTTO

450 g (1 lb) pork sausages
100 g (4 oz) streaky bacon, rinded and chopped
1 onion, peeled and chopped
2 celery sticks, scrubbed and thinly sliced
2 courgettes, trimmed and cut into thin strips
350 g (12 oz) long-grain rice
2 tablespoons tomato purée
600 ml (1 pint) boiling chicken stock
½ teaspoon dried oregano
salt
freshly ground black pepper
1 tablespoon chopped fresh parsley

Power Setting: Full/Maximum
Preparation and Cooking Time: 40 minutes

1. Place the sausages on a plate or microwave grill rack and prick thoroughly with a fork. Cook for 5-6 minutes, turning and re-arranging the sausage once.
2. Place the bacon in a large bowl and cook for 3 minutes, stirring once. Add the onion and celery. Cover and cook for 4 minutes, stirring once.
3. Add the courgettes, rice, tomato purée, chicken stock, oregano and salt and pepper to taste, blending well. Cover and cook for 13 minutes, stirring twice. Leave to stand, covered, for 10 minutes.
4. Meanwhile, cut the sausages into bite-size pieces. Stir into the risotto mixture with the parsley. Serve at once.

FREEZING DETAILS
1. Prepare the recipe to the end of step 4.
2. Cool quickly and pack into a rigid container. Cover, seal, label and freeze for up to 3 months.
REHEATING DETAILS
Power Setting: Defrost and Full/Maximum
Defrosting and Cooking Time: 25-27 minutes
1. Remove all wrappings and place the frozen risotto in a bowl. Cook on defrost power for 8-10 minutes, breaking up the risotto with a fork every 3 minutes. Leave to stand for 10 minutes.
2. Cook on full/maximum power for 7 minutes, stirring once.

SAVOURY MUFFIN TOPPERS

1 × 100 g (4 oz) jar tomato paste with basil or 1 × 141 g
  (5 oz) can tomato purée and 2 teaspoons dried basil
100 g (4 oz) garlic sausage, cubed
1 clove garlic, peeled and crushed
1 small onion, peeled and grated
4 large muffins, halved and toasted
175 g (6 oz) Cheddar cheese, grated
1 × 56 g (2 oz) can anchovy fillets, drained
To garnish:
black olives

Power Setting: Full/Maximum
Preparation and Cooking Time: 10-15 minutes

1. Place the tomato paste with basil, or purée and dried basil, in a bowl with the garlic sausage, garlic and onion. Cover and cook for 4 minutes, stirring once.
2. Place the muffin slices, cut side up on paper towels, on a large microwave baking tray and spread evenly with the tomato mixture. Top with the grated cheese.
3. Arrange a lattice of anchovy fillets on top and garnish with black olives.
4. To serve immediately, cook for 4 minutes, re-arranging the muffins twice so that they cook evenly.

FREEZING DETAILS
1. Prepare the recipe to the end of step 3.
2. Cool quickly, then open-freeze until firm.
3. Pack in a rigid box, interleaved with freezer film. Cover, seal, label and freeze for up to 1 month.
REHEATING DETAILS
Power Setting: Full/Maximum
Defrosting and Cooking Time: 4-6 minutes
Remove all wrappings and place the muffins on paper towels on a microwave baking tray. Cook for 4-6 minutes, re-arranging the muffins twice, until hot, bubbly and heated through.

Sausage risotto;
Savoury muffin toppers

SWEET AND SOUR SOUP

2 tablespoons oil
450 g (1 lb) lean pork, finely chopped
25 g (1 oz) plain flour
salt
freshly ground black pepper
1 onion, peeled and chopped
1 green pepper, cored, seeded and chopped
1 large carrot, peeled and grated
1 × 397 g (14 oz) can peeled tomatoes
300 ml (½ pint) white meat stock
1 tablespoon red wine vinegar
1 garlic clove, peeled and crushed
grated rind of 1 orange
1 tablespoon tomato purée
½ teaspoon ground ginger

Power Setting: Full/Maximum
Preparation and Cooking Time: 40 minutes

1. Preheat a browning dish for 8 minutes (or according to the manufacturer's instructions). Brush with the oil and cook for a further 1 minute.
2. Toss the pork in the flour with salt and pepper to taste. Add the pork to the browning dish and turn quickly on all sides to brown evenly. Add the onion, green pepper and carrot, cover and cook for 8 minutes, stirring once.
3. Transfer to a large bowl and stir in the tomatoes with their juice, stock, vinegar, garlic, orange rind, tomato purée and ginger. Add salt and pepper to taste. Cover and cook for 15 minutes, stirring twice.
4. Serve hot with crusty bread.

FREEZING DETAILS
1. Prepare the recipe to the end of step 3.
2. Cool quickly, transfer to a rigid container, allowing 2.5 cm (1 inch) headspace. Cover, seal, label and freeze for up to 2 months.
REHEATING DETAILS
Power Setting: Defrost and Full/Maximum
Defrosting and Cooking Time: 32 minutes
1. Remove all wrappings and place the frozen soup in a suitable serving dish. Cook on defrost power for 12 minutes, breaking up and stirring twice. Leave to stand for 10 minutes.
2. Cover and cook on full/maximum power for 10 minutes, stirring twice.
3. Serve hot with crusty bread.

SMOKED HADDOCK WITH NOODLES

1 small onion, peeled
6 cloves
1 bay leaf
6 peppercorns
1 small carrot, peeled
300 ml (½ pint) milk
2 × 198 g (7 oz) packets frozen buttered smoked haddock
40 g (1½ oz) butter
40 g (1½ oz) plain flour
2 teaspoons chopped fresh parsley
75 g (3 oz) grated cheese
225 g (8 oz) noodles or tagliatelle
600 ml (1 pint) boiling water
1 tablespoon oil
To garnish:
lemon slices
tomato slices
sprigs of fresh parsley

Power Setting: Defrost and Full/Maximum
Preparation and Cooking Time: 40 minutes

1. Stud the onion with cloves and place in a bowl with the bay leaf, peppercorns, carrot and milk. Cook on defrost power for 10-11 minutes until hot. Leave to stand while cooking the haddock.
2. Pierce the packets of smoked haddock and place on a plate. Cook on full/maximum power for 10 minutes, shaking the packets gently after 6 minutes.

Sweet and sour soup; Pork rolls with cabbage

3. Place the butter in a jug and cook on full power for ½ minute to melt. Add the flour, mixing well. Gradually add the strained milk and cook on full/maximum power for 2-2½ minutes, stirring every 1 minute until the sauce is smooth and thickened. Stir in the parsley and the cheese until melted.

4. Place the noodles, water and oil in a deep container. Cover and cook on full/maximum power for 6 minutes. Leave to stand for 3 minutes, then drain.

5. Flake the haddock into bite-sized pieces, removing and discarding any skin. Stir into the sauce, tossing gently to mix.

6. To serve immediately, arrange the noodles round the edge of a shallow serving dish. Spoon the haddock mixture into the centre. Garnish with lemon slices, tomato slices and parsley sprigs.

FREEZING DETAILS

1. Prepare the recipe to the end of step 5.

2. Cool quickly, pack the noodles and haddock mixture separately into rigid containers. Cover, seal, label and freeze for up to 2 months.

REHEATING DETAILS

Power Setting: Defrost and Full/Maximum

Defrosting and Cooking Time: 30-31 minutes

1. Remove all wrappings. Cook the haddock mixture on defrost power for 8 minutes. Leave to stand for 5 minutes.

2. Cook the noodles on defrost power for 6 minutes. Leave to stand for 2 minutes.

3. Cook the haddock mixture on full/maximum power for 5-6 minutes, stirring once.

4. Cook the noodles on full/maximum power for 4 minutes. Serve as in step 6 above.

PORK ROLLS WITH CABBAGE

450 g (1 lb) pork sausage meat
1 onion, peeled and chopped
100 g (4 oz) button mushrooms, chopped
1 tablespoon lemon juice
grated rind of ½ lemon
1 teaspoon mustard powder
2 tablespoons chopped fresh parsley
1 egg, beaten
salt
freshly ground black pepper
1 medium cabbage, washed and shredded
4 tablespoons water
1 tablespoon soy sauce
1 tablespoon oil
To garnish:
tomato wedges
sprig of fresh parsley

Power Setting: Full/Maximum
Preparation and Cooking Time: 50 minutes

1. Mix the sausage meat with the onion, mushrooms, lemon juice, lemon rind, mustard, parsley, egg and salt and pepper to taste, blending well. Divide and shape into 8 portions.

2. Place the cabbage in a bowl with the water and salt to taste. Cover and cook for 8 minutes, stirring once. Drain and toss with the soy sauce.

3. If serving immediately, pre-heat a large browning dish for 8 minutes (or according to the manufacturer's instructions). Brush with the oil and cook for a further 1 minute.

4. Add the pork rolls and turn quickly on all sides to brown evenly. Cook for 7-8 minutes, turning and re-arranging the rolls once. Serve on a bed of the seasoned cabbage and garnish with tomato wedges and parsley.

FREEZING DETAILS

1. Prepare the cabbage mixture and the uncooked pork rolls to the end of step 2.

2. Cool quickly, pack the cooked cabbage mixture in a rigid container. Cover, seal and label.

3. Freeze the uncooked pork rolls interleaved between freezer film and overwrapped with aluminium foil. Seal, label and freeze both for up to 3 months.

REHEATING DETAILS

Power Setting: Defrost and Full/Maximum

Defrosting and Cooking Time: 28-32 minutes

1. Remove all wrappings. Place the pork rolls on a plate and cook on defrost power for 6-7 minutes, turning and re-arranging once. Leave to stand while cooking the cabbage.

2. Place the frozen cabbage in a bowl. Cover and cook on full/maximum power for 4-6 minutes, stirring frequently.

3. Cook the pork rolls as in steps 3 and 4 above. Reheat the cabbage on full/maximum power for 2 minutes if necessary.

4. Serve the pork rolls on the bed of cooked cabbage and garnish with tomato wedges and parsley.

PASTA SCALLOPS

175 g (6 oz) pasta shells
750 ml (1¼ pints) boiling water
1 tablespoon oil
salt
6 rashers streaky bacon, rinded
20 g (¾ oz) butter
20 g (¾ oz) plain flour
300 ml (½ pint) milk
freshly ground black pepper
75 g (3 oz) grated cheese
2 hard-boiled eggs, shelled
To garnish:
sprigs of fresh parsley

Power Setting: Full/Maximum
Preparation and Cooking Time: 30 minutes

1. Place the pasta in a deep dish with the water, oil and salt to taste. Cover and cook for 12-14 minutes, stirring once. Leave to stand while cooking the bacon and sauce.
2. Place the rashers on a plate or microwave bacon rack, cover with a paper towel and cook for 3 minutes until crisp.
3. Place the butter in a jug and cook for ½ minute to melt. Add the flour, blending well. Gradually add the milk and cook for 3½-4 minutes, stirring every 1 minute until smooth and thickened. Add salt and pepper to taste.
4. Stir in two-thirds of the cheese until melted.
5. Chop the eggs coarsely and mix with the hot drained pasta and salt and pepper to taste.
6. Arrange the pasta mixture in 4 deep scallop shells. Spoon over the sauce. Crumble the bacon coarsely and sprinkle over the sauce.
7. To serve immediately, cook for 2-3 minutes, re-arranging the shells twice.
8. Brown under a preheated hot grill if wished. Garnish with fresh parsley.

FREEZING DETAILS
1. Prepare the recipe to the end of step 6.
2. Cool quickly, cover, seal, label and freeze for up to 3 months.
REHEATING DETAILS
Power Setting: Defrost and Full/Maximum
Defrosting and Cooking Time: 23-24 minutes
1. Remove all wrappings and cook the scallops on defrost power for 10 minutes. Leave to stand for 10 minutes.
2. Cook on full/maximum power for 3-4 minutes, re-arranging the shells twice.
3. Brown under a preheated hot grill if wished. Garnish with fresh parsley.

LEEK AND LUNCHEON SAUSAGE SUPPER

8 medium leeks, trimmed and washed
4 tablespoons water
8 slices luncheon sausage
25 g (1 oz) butter
25 g (1 oz) plain flour
300 ml (½ pint) milk
100 g (4 oz) Cheddar cheese, grated
salt
freshly ground black pepper

Power Setting: Full/Maximum
Preparation and Cooking Time: 25 minutes

1. Place the leeks in a dish. Add the water, cover and cook for 10-12 minutes until tender, stirring once. Drain thoroughly.
2. Wrap each leek in a slice of the luncheon sausage and place in a flameproof serving dish.
3. Place the butter in a jug and cook for ½ minute to melt. Add the flour, blending well. Gradually add the milk and cook for 3½-4 minutes, stirring every 1 minute until smooth and thickened.
4. Stir in three-quarters of the cheese until melted. Add salt and pepper to taste. Spoon over the leeks and sprinkle with the remaining cheese.
5. If serving immediately, cook for 2-3 minutes until hot and bubbly.
6. Brown under a preheated hot grill if wished.

FREEZING DETAILS
1. Prepare the recipe to the end of step 4.
2. Cool quickly, cover, seal, label and freeze for up to 3 months.
REHEATING DETAILS
Power Setting: Defrost and Full/Maximum
Defrosting and Cooking Time: 18-21 minutes
1. Remove all wrappings and cook the rolls on defrost power for 8 minutes. Leave to stand for 5 minutes.
2. Cook on full/maximum power for 5-8 minutes.
3. Brown under a preheated hot grill if wished.

CLOCKWISE FROM LEFT:
Pasta scallops; Salami-stuffed pasta;
Leek and luncheon sausage supper

SALAMI-STUFFED PASTA

6 sheets lasagne
2 teaspoons oil
900 ml (1½ pints) boiling water
salt
Filling:
1 large onion, peeled and chopped
100 g (4 oz) mushrooms, sliced
225 g (8 oz) salami, diced
1 × 425 g (15 oz) can tomatoes
1½ tablespoons cornflour
Topping:
50 g (2 oz) butter
50g (2 oz) plain flour
600 ml (1 pint) milk
175 g (6 oz) grated cheese
To garnish:
fresh bay leaves

Power Setting: Full/Maximum
Preparation and Cooking Time: 50 minutes

1. Place the lasagne in a deep rectangular dish. Add 1 teaspoon oil, the water and salt to taste. Cover and cook for 9 minutes. Leave to stand for 10 minutes, drain and rinse in cold water.
2. Place the remaining oil and onion in a bowl. Cover and cook for 3 minutes. Add the mushrooms, cover and cook for 2 minutes.

3. Stir in three-quarters of the salami and the tomatoes, blending well. Cover and cook for 3 minutes, stirring twice.
4. Mix the cornflour with a little water and stir into the salami mixture. Cook for 2 minutes, stirring once, until thickened.
5. Cut the cooked lasagne sheets in half. Spoon equal quantities of the salami mixture on the pieces of pasta, roll up to enclose and place, seam side down, in a large gratin dish.
6. Place the butter in a jug and cook for 1 minute to melt. Add the flour, blending well. Gradually add the milk and cook for 5½-6 minutes, stirring every 1 minute until smooth and thickened. Stir in two-thirds of the cheese until melted.
7. Pour the sauce over the pasta, sprinkle with the remaining cheese and salami.
8. To serve immediately, cook for 2-3 minutes, turning the dish once, or until heated through. Brown under a preheated hot grill if wished. Garnish with bay leaves.

FREEZING DETAILS
1. Prepare the recipe to the end of step 7.
2. Cool quickly, cover, seal, label and freeze for up to 2 months.
REHEATING DETAILS
Power Setting: Defrost and Full/Maximum
Defrosting and Cooking Time: 29-31 minutes
1. Remove all wrappings and cook the pasta on defrost power for 15 minutes. Leave to stand for 10 minutes.
2. Cook on full/maximum power for 4-6 minutes, turning the dish twice. Brown under a preheated hot grill if wished. Garnish with bay leaves.

CHEESE AND HAM TOASTIES

8 small slices thin white bread, crusts removed
1-2 teaspoons wholegrain mustard
4 slices quick-melting processed cheese
4 slices cooked ham
40 g (1 ½ oz) butter

Power Setting: Full/Maximum
Preparation and Cooking Time: 20 minutes

1. Spread half the bread slices with mustard to taste. Top each with a slice of cheese and ham. Cover with the remaining bread slices, pressing down well.
2. To serve immediately, place the butter in a bowl and cook for 1 minute to melt.
3. Preheat a large browning dish for 8 minutes (or according to the manufacturer's instructions).
4. Brush one side of each sandwich with half the butter. Place in the browning dish and allow to brown on the underside, about 1-2 minutes.
5. Quickly brush the second side of each sandwich with the remaining butter, turn over with tongs and cook for 2 minutes, turning the dish once.
6. Cut each sandwich in half diagonally to serve (with napkins).

FREEZING DETAILS
1. Prepare the recipe to the end of step 1.
2. Freeze the uncooked sandwiches, wrapped in aluminium foil, sealed and labelled for up to 3 months.
REHEATING DETAILS
Power Setting: Defrost and Full/Maximum
Defrosting and Cooking Time: 22-23 minutes
1. Remove all wrappings, place on a plate and cook on defrost power for 5 minutes. Leave to stand for 5 minutes.
2. Cook as in steps 2-6 above. Serve hot with napkins.

DANISH PIZZA

Serves 2

8 rashers streaky bacon, rinded
50 g (2 oz) butter
1 onion, peeled and chopped
1 × 227 g (8 oz) can peeled tomatoes, drained and chopped
pinch of dried mixed herbs
salt
freshly ground black pepper
100 g (4 oz) self-raising flour
water to mix
1 tablespoon oil
100 g (4 oz) Samsoe cheese, sliced
3 stuffed olives, sliced

To garnish:

a few sprigs of fresh herbs, e.g. rosemary

Power Setting: Full/Maximum
Preparation and Cooking Time: 45 minutes

1. Place the bacon on a plate or microwave bacon rack, cover with a paper towel and cook for 3¼-4 minutes, until crisp
2. Place half the butter in a bowl and cook for ½ minute to melt. Add the onion, cover and cook for 2½ minutes. Add the tomatoes, herbs and salt and pepper to taste. Cover and cook for 4 minutes, stirring twice.

SPAGHETTI MOZZARELLA

225 g (8 oz) spaghetti
1.2 litres (2 pints) boiling water
1 tablespoon oil
salt
100 g (4 oz) butter
1 garlic clove, peeled and crushed
4 tomatoes, peeled, seeded and quartered
75 g (3 oz) black olives
175 g (6 oz) Mozzarella cheese, cubed
3 tablespoons chopped fresh parsley
freshly ground black pepper

Power Setting: Full/Maximum
Preparation and Cooking Time: 25 minutes

1. Wind the spaghetti into a deep dish with the water, oil and salt to taste until softened. Submerge in the water, cover and cook for

3. To make the dough, rub the remaining butter into the flour and gradually add about 3-4 tablespoons of water to make a soft dough. Knead lightly until smooth and roll out on a lightly floured surface to a square large enough to fit a small browning dish.
4. Preheat the browning dish for 6 minutes (or according to the manufacturer's instructions). Brush with the oil and heat for a further ½ minute.
5. Place the dough in the browning dish and top with the tomato mixture, spreading it evenly. Arrange the cheese on top and cook for 5½ minutes, turning the dish every 1 minute.
6. Arrange the cooked bacon rashers on top of the pizza to form a lattice. Place the sliced olives in the 'window' of each lattice.
7. To serve immediately, cook for a further ½ minute. Leave to stand for 5 minutes, then remove from the dish and garnish with rosemary. Serve with a crisp salad if wished.

FREEZING DETAILS
1. Prepare the recipe to the end of step 6.
2. Cool quickly, place in a rigid container, cover, seal, label and freeze for up to 2 months.
REHEATING DETAILS
Power Setting: Full/Maximum
Defrosting and Cooking Time: 6 minutes
1. Remove all wrappings. Place the pizza on a double thickness piece of paper towel. Cook for 6 minutes until the pizza is hot and bubbly.
2. Serve garnished with rosemary and with a crisp salad if wished.

about 10 minutes. Leave to stand for 5 minutes.
2. To serve immediately, place the butter in a bowl and cook for about 3-4 minutes, until 'nutty'. Add the garlic and cook for ½ minute.
3. Drain the cooked spaghetti and toss in the hot garlic butter with the tomatoes, olives, cheese, parsley and salt and pepper to taste. Serve at once on warmed plates with a simple green salad.

FREEZING DETAILS
1. Prepare the recipe to the end of step 1.
2. Place in a rigid container, cover, seal, label and freeze for up to 1 month.
REHEATING DETAILS
Power Setting: Defrost and Full/Maximum
Defrosting and Cooking Time: 18-19 minutes
1. Remove all wrappings. Place the pasta in a bowl, cover and cook on defrost power for 6½ minutes. Leave to stand for 2 minutes.
2. Cook on full/maximum power for 4 minutes. Leave to stand for 2 minutes.
3. Continue from step 2 above.

Danish pizza;
Cheese and ham toasties

PASTA AND TUNA SALAD

225 g (8 oz) pasta bows or shells
900 ml (1 ½ pints) boiling water
1 tablespoon oil
salt
1 × 200 g (7 oz) can tuna in oil
1 green pepper, cored, seeded and chopped
4 celery sticks, scrubbed and chopped
100 g (4 oz) black olives, stoned
Dressing:
2 tablespoons chive mustard
2 tablespoons white wine vinegar
2 tablespoons single cream
freshly ground black pepper
To garnish:
radish slices

Power Setting: Full/Maximum
Preparation and Cooking Time: 25 minutes

1. Place the pasta in a deep dish with the water, oil and salt to taste. Cover and cook for 12-14 minutes. Leave to stand for 5 minutes. Drain well, rinse with cold water and drain again.
2. Drain the oil from the tuna and reserve. Flake the tuna into chunks and add to the pasta with the pepper, celery and olives, tossing well to mix.
3. If serving immediately, blend the reserved tuna oil with the chive mustard, vinegar, cream and salt and pepper to taste. Toss with the salad ingredients. Serve at once, garnished with a circle of radish slices. If freezing the salad do not prepare the dressing until later and discard the tuna oil.

FREEZING DETAILS
1. Prepare the recipe to the end of step 2.
2. Pack the salad in a rigid container. Cover, seal, label and freeze for up to 1 month.
DEFROSTING DETAILS
Power Setting: Defrost
Defrosting Time: 13 minutes
1. Remove all wrappings. Cook on defrost power for 8 minutes, stirring twice. Leave to stand for 5 minutes.
2. Prepare the dressing as in step 3 above, using 3 tablespoons salad oil instead of the tuna oil. Toss with the salad ingredients. Serve at once, garnished with a circle of radish slices.

Pasta and tuna salad;
Simple country-style pâté

SIMPLE COUNTRY-STYLE PÂTÉ

450 g (1 lb) pig's liver
450 g (1 lb) belly of pork
1 onion, peeled
1 garlic clove, peeled
2 eggs, beaten
2 tablespoons sherry
salt
freshly ground black pepper
225 g (8 oz) rashers streaky bacon, rinded
To garnish:
cucumber slices
tomato slices
sprigs of fresh parsley

Power Setting: Defrost
Preparation and Cooking Time: 40 minutes, plus chilling

1. Mince the liver with the pork, onion and garlic. Add the eggs, sherry and salt and pepper to taste, blending well.
2. Stretch the bacon with the back of a knife and use to line a medium terrine dish.
3. Spoon in the pâté mixture, cover and cook for 25 minutes.
4. Leave to cool in the dish, then chill for 4-6 hours or overnight.
5. To serve immediately, turn the pâté out of the terrine and garnish with cucumber, tomato and parsley. Serve sliced with crusty bread.

FREEZING DETAILS
1. Prepare the recipe to the end of step 3.
2. Cool quickly, cover the dish, seal, label and freeze for up to 2 months.
DEFROSTING DETAILS
Power Setting: Defrost
Defrosting Time: 40 minutes
1. Remove all wrappings and cook on defrost power for 10 minutes. Leave to stand for 30 minutes.
2. Turn the pâté out of the terrine and garnish with cucumber, tomato and parsley. Serve sliced with crusty bread.

Variation:
Tropical-style Pâté: Prepare and cook the pâté as above but add the finely grated rind of ½ orange and use 2 tablespoons tropical or mandarin fruit juice, or orange-flavoured liqueur (e.g. Curaçao), instead of the sherry.

SPEEDY CHILLI CON CARNE

1 tablespoon oil
1 onion, peeled and chopped
1 red pepper, cored, seeded and chopped
675 g (1½ lb) minced beef
1 × 225 g (8 oz) can peeled tomatoes
2 tablespoons tomato purée
1 tablespoon red wine vinegar
1 tablespoon chilli seasoning or mild chilli powder
1 teaspoon sugar
salt
1 × 450 g (1 lb) can baked beans in tomato sauce

Power Setting: Full/Maximum
Preparation and Cooking Time: 55 minutes

1. Place the oil, onion and pepper in a bowl. Cover and cook for 5 minutes, stirring once.
2. Add the beef, blending well. Cook for 7 minutes, stirring and breaking up the beef twice.
3. Add the tomatoes with their juice, tomato purée, vinegar, chilli seasoning, sugar and salt to taste, blending well. Cover and cook for 30 minutes, stirring twice.
4. Add the beans, mixing well to blend. Cover and cook for 7 minutes, stirring once.
5. Serve with boiled rice or crusty bread.

FREEZING DETAILS
1. Prepare the recipe to the end of step 4.
2. Cool quickly and spoon into a rigid container. Cover, seal, label and freeze for up to 3 months.
REHEATING DETAILS
Power Setting: Defrost and Full/Maximum
Defrosting and Cooking Time: 32-33 minutes
1. Remove all wrappings and place the frozen mixture in a bowl. Cook on defrost power for 16 minutes, stirring twice. Allow to stand for 10 minutes.
2. Cook on full/maximum power for 6-7 minutes until hot and bubbling. Serve with boiled rice or crusty bread.

Variation:
Speedy Calypso Chilli Con Carne: Prepare and cook as above but use 1 × 425 g (15 oz) can Calypso beans (red kidney beans in a tangy tropical barbecue sauce) instead of the baked beans in tomato sauce.

BEAN-STUFFED PEPPERS

Serves 6

1 tablespoon oil
1 onion, peeled and chopped
450 g (1 lb) minced beef
5 tablespoons beef stock
1 tablespoon tomato purée
100 g (4 oz) button mushrooms, chopped
salt
freshly ground black pepper
2 medium red peppers
2 medium green peppers
2 medium yellow peppers
1 × 450 g (1 lb) can baked beans in tomato sauce
1 × 225 g (8 oz) can chopped tomatoes
1 garlic clove, peeled and crushed
1 teaspoon dried mixed herbs.

To garnish:
sprigs of fresh rosemary

Power Setting: Full/Maximum
Preparation and Cooking Time: about 45 minutes

1. Place the oil and onion in a large bowl. Cover and cook for 3 minutes.
2. Add the beef, blending well. Cook for 9 minutes, stirring and breaking up the beef twice.
3. Add the stock, tomato purée, mushrooms and salt and pepper to taste. Cover and cook for 8 minutes, stirring once.
4. Meanwhile, cut a slice from the top of each pepper. Remove and discard the core and seeds. Place the peppers in a bowl, cover and cook for 4½ minutes, turn over and cook for 4½ minutes.
5. Blend the meat mixture with the beans. Stand the peppers upright in a shallow dish and fill with the bean and beef mixture.
6. Mix the tomatoes with the garlic and herbs and spoon around the peppers. Cover and cook for 8-10 minutes. Garnish with rosemary and serve.

FREEZING DETAILS
1. Prepare the recipe to the end of step 6.
2. Cool quickly, cover, seal, label and freeze for up to 3 months.
REHEATING DETAILS
Power Setting: Defrost and Full/Maximum
Defrosting and Cooking Time: 45-47 minutes
1. Remove all wrappings and cook on defrost power for 35 minutes.
2. Cook on full/maximum power for 10-12 minutes. Garnish.

CAULIFLOWER AND MACARONI CHEESE

1 small cauliflower, trimmed and cut into florets
8 tablespoons water
225 g (8 oz) quick-cooking macaroni
600 ml (1 pint) boiling water
175 g (6 oz) streaky bacon, rinded and chopped
25 g (1 oz) butter
25 g (1 oz) plain flour
350 ml (12 fl oz) milk
2 teaspoons chive mustard
salt
freshly ground black pepper
75 g (3 oz) grated cheese
To garnish
1 tomato, sliced
sprigs of fresh parsley

Power Setting: Full/Maximum
Preparation and Cooking Time: 35-40 minutes

1. Place the cauliflower florets and cold water in a bowl. Cover and cook for 10 minutes, stirring once. Drain thoroughly.
2. Place the macaroni in a deep bowl with the boiling water. Cover and cook for 7 minutes. Allow to stand for 3 minutes, then drain thoroughly.
3. Place the bacon in a bowl. Cook for 4 minutes, stirring once. Drain thoroughly.
4. Place the butter in a large jug and cook for ½ minute to melt. Add the flour, blending well. Gradually add the milk and cook for 4-5 minutes, stirring every 1 minute until smooth and thickened. Stir in the chive mustard, salt and pepper to taste and cheese until melted.
5. Toss the cauliflower, macaroni and bacon in the sauce and spoon into a serving dish.
6. To serve immediately, cook for 2-3 minutes to reheat and serve garnished with tomato slices and chopped parsley.

FREEZING DETAILS
1. Prepare the recipe to the end of step 5.
2. Cool quickly, cover, seal, label and freeze for up to 3 months.
REHEATING DETAILS
Power Setting: Defrost and Full/Maximum
Defrosting and Cooking Time: 28-34 minutes
1. Remove all wrappings. Cook on defrost power for 25-30 minutes until thoroughly thawed.
2. Cook on full/maximum power for 3-4 minutes. Serve garnished with tomato slices and chopped parsley.

BROCCOLI AND CHICKEN BAKE

350 g (12 oz) broccoli spears, trimmed
4 tablespoons water
salt
225 g (8 oz) cooked chicken, cut into thin strips
Béchamel sauce:
1 small onion, peeled and halved
1 carrot, peeled and sliced
1 bay leaf
12 peppercorns
few sprigs of fresh parsley
300 ml (½ pint) milk
25 g (1 oz) butter
25 g (1 oz) plain flour
freshly ground black pepper
To garnish:
50 g (2 oz) toasted flaked almonds

Power Setting: Full/Maximum and Defrost
Preparation and Cooking Time: 30 minutes

1. Place the broccoli spears in a shallow flameproof dish with the water and a pinch of salt, arranging the stalks to the outside of the dish and the florets to the centre. Cover and cook on full/maximum power for 6 minutes. Drain thoroughly.
2. Add the chicken and mix well.
3. Meanwhile, place the onion, carrot, bay leaf, peppercorns, parsley and milk in a large jug. Cook on defrost power for 10-11 minutes until hot. Strain.
4. Place the butter in another jug and cook on full/maximum for ½ minute to melt. Stir in the flour and salt and pepper to taste.
5. Gradually add the strained milk and cook on full/maximum power for 1½-2 minutes, stirring every ½ minute, until smooth and thickened. Pour over the broccoli and chicken mixture.
6. To serve immediately, cover and cook on full/maximum power for 3-4 minutes, turning the dish twice. Sprinkle with the almonds and serve at once.

FREEZING DETAILS
1. Prepare the recipe to the end of step 5.
2. Cool quickly, cover, seal, label and freeze for up to 3 months.
REHEATING DETAILS
Power Setting: Defrost and Full/Maximum
Defrosting and Cooking Time: 29-31 minutes.
1. Remove all wrappings. Cook on defrost power for 20 minutes. Leave to stand for 5 minutes.
2. Cook on full/maximum power for 4-6 minutes. Sprinkle with the almonds and serve at once. Brown under a preheated grill if wished.

FROM TOP RIGHT, CLOCKWISE:
Cauliflower and macaroni cheese;
Bean-stuffed peppers;
Broccoli and chicken bake

HERDER'S PIE

25 g (1 oz) butter
1 large onion, peeled and chopped
100 g (4 oz) button mushrooms, quartered
1 × 175 g (6 oz) can pimientos, drained and chopped
1 × 400 g (14 oz) can peeled tomatoes, drained
450 g (1 lb) cooked bacon or ham, coarsely minced or finely
    chopped
1 tablespoon plain flour
2 tablespoons tomato ketchup
1 tablespoon Worcestershire sauce
½ teaspoon dried rosemary
freshly ground black pepper

Topping:
675 g (1 ½ lb) potatoes, peeled and cubed
1 large carrot, peeled and grated
5 tablespoons water
25 g (1 oz) butter
50 g (2 oz) cheese, grated

Power Setting: Full/Maximum
Preparation and Cooking Time: 40 minutes

1. Place the butter in a large bowl with the onion and mushrooms, cover and cook for 5 minutes, stirring once.
2. Add the pimientos, tomatoes, bacon or ham tossed in the flour, tomato ketchup, Worcestershire sauce, rosemary and pepper to taste, blending well. Cover and cook for 10 minutes, stirring twice. Spoon into a large shallow dish.
3. Place the potatoes and carrot in a bowl with the water. Cover and cook for 12-14 minutes until tender. Drain and mash with the butter and cheese. Pipe or spoon over the meat mixture to cover. If piping the mixture, spoon into a piping bag fitted with a large star-shaped nozzle.
4. To serve immediately, cook for 6 minutes, turning the dish every 1 ½ minutes.
5. Brown under a preheated hot grill if preferred.

FREEZING DETAILS
1. Prepare the recipe to the end of step 3.
2. Cool quickly, cover, seal, label and freeze up to 3 months.
REHEATING DETAILS
Power Setting: Defrost and Full/Maximum
Defrosting and Cooking Time: 40 minutes
1. Remove all wrappings. Cook on defrost power for 10 minutes. Allow to stand for 10 minutes. Cook on defrost power for a further 10 minutes.
2. Cook on full/maximum power for 10 minutes to reheat, turning every 2 minutes.
3. Brown under a preheated hot grill if wished.

HAM AND POTATO SUPPER

50 g (2 oz) butter
2 onions, peeled and chopped
2 teaspoons Meaux mustard
2 teaspoons chopped fresh tarragon or 1 teaspoon dried
    tarragon
3 tablespoons plain flour
300 ml (½ pint) milk
300 ml (½ pint) white meat stock
675 g (1 ½ lb) cooked ham, cubed
900 g (2 lb) potatoes, peeled and cubed
8 tablespoons water
2 tablespoons milk
pinch of ground nutmeg
salt
freshly ground black pepper

Power Setting: Full/Maximum
Preparation and Cooking Time: 50 minutes

1. Place half the butter in a bowl with the onion. Cover and cook for 4 minutes.
2. Stir in the mustard, tarragon and flour, blending well. Gradually add the milk and stock. Cook for 8-9 minutes, stirring every 2 minutes until smooth and thickened. Fold in the cubed ham.
3. Place the potatoes in a bowl with the water. Cover and cook for 16-18 minutes until tender. Drain and mash with the remaining butter, milk, nutmeg and salt and pepper to taste.
4. Spoon the ham mixture into a large dish. Spoon the potato mixture into a piping bag fitted with a large star-shaped nozzle and pipe round the edge to make a border.
5. To serve immediately, cook for 4 minutes, turning the dish every 1 minute.
6. Brown under a preheated hot grill if wished.

FREEZING DETAILS
1. Prepare the recipe to the end of step 4
2. Cool quickly, cover, seal, label and freeze for up to 3 months.
REHEATING DETAILS
Power Setting: Defrost and Full/Maximum
Defrosting and Cooking Time: 40-42 minutes
1. Remove all wrappings. Cook on defrost power for 20 minutes. Allow to stand for 10 minutes.
2. Cook on full/maximum power for 10-12 minutes, turning the dish every 2 minutes.
3. Brown under a preheated hot grill if wished.

FROM LEFT TO RIGHT:
Herder's pie; Ham and
potato supper; Wholewheat
spinach and cheese quiche

WHOLEWHEAT SPINACH AND CHEESE QUICHE

175 g (6 oz) wholewheat flour
pinch of salt
40 g (1½ oz) lard
40 g (1½ oz) margarine
2 tablespoons iced water
Filling:
450 g (1 lb) fresh spinach leaves or 1 × 225 g (8 oz) packet
*   frozen leaf spinach*
100 g (4 oz) cottage cheese
2 eggs, beaten
75 ml (2½ fl oz) single cream
4 tablespoons grated Parmesan cheese
salt
freshly ground black pepper

Power Setting: Full/Maximum and Defrost
Preparation and Cooking Time: about 1 hour

1. Mix the flour with the salt in a bowl. Rub in the lard and margarine with the fingertips until the mixture resembles fine breadcrumbs. Add the water and bind together to a firm but pliable dough. Turn on to a lightly floured surface and knead until smooth and free from cracks.
2. Roll out the pastry on a lightly floured surface to a round large enough to line a 20 cm (8 inch) dish. Press in firmly, taking care not to stretch the pastry. Cut the pastry away, leaving a 5mm (¼ inch) 'collar' above the dish to allow for any shrinkage that may occur (page 37). Prick the base and sides well with a fork.
3. Place a double thickness layer of paper towel over the base, easing it into position round the edges.
4. Cook on full/maximum power for 3½ minutes, giving the dish a quarter turn every 1 minute. Remove the paper and cook on full/maximum power for a further 1½ minutes.
5. Place the fresh spinach in a bowl, cover and cook for 5-7 minutes. Drain thoroughly and chop coarsely. Alternatively, cook the frozen spinach for 6-7 minutes, breaking up the spinach after 3 minutes. Drain thoroughly and chop coarsely.
6. Mix together the cottage cheese, eggs, cream, Parmesan cheese and salt and pepper. Stir in the spinach, blending well. Spoon into the flan case and cook on defrost power for 14-16 minutes, giving the dish a quarter turn every 3 minutes. Allow to stand for 10-15 minutes. The flan should set completely during this time.

FREEZING DETAILS
1. Prepare the recipe to the end of step 6.
2. Cool quickly, pack into a rigid container, cover, seal, label and freeze for up to 2 months.
REHEATING DETAILS
Power Setting: Full/Maximum
Defrosting and Cooking Time: 9-10 minutes
1. Remove all wrappings. Cook on full/maximum power for 4-5 minutes, turning once. Allow to stand for 3 minutes to serve cold.
2. To reheat, cook on full/maximum for 2 minutes.

BACON RATATOUILLE

2 tablespoons oil
275 g (10 oz) streaky bacon, rinded and chopped
1 large onion, peeled and chopped
2 garlic cloves, peeled and crushed (optional)
2 green peppers, cored, seeded and sliced
225 g (8 oz) tomatoes, peeled and sliced
450 g (1 lb) courgettes, sliced
50 g (2 oz) mushrooms, chopped
1 teaspoon dried thyme
2 tablespoons tomato purée
salt
freshly ground black pepper
grated Parmesan cheese, to serve

Power Setting: Full/Maximum
Preparation and Cooking Time: 35 minutes

1. Place the oil in a large bowl and cook for 1 minute. Add the bacon, cover and cook for 8 minutes, stirring twice. Remove the bacon with a slotted spoon and set aside.
2. Add the onion, garlic (if used) and peppers to the bowl. Cover and cook for 6 minutes, stirring once.
3. Add the tomatoes, courgettes, mushrooms, thyme, tomato purée and salt and pepper to taste, blending well. Cover and cook for 7 minutes, stirring once.
4. Add the bacon, mixing well. Cover and cook for a further 6 minutes, stirring once. Serve hot or cold, sprinkled with Parmesan cheese.

FREEZING DETAILS
1. Prepare the recipe to the end of step 4 but do not add the Parmesan cheese.
2. Cool quickly, cover, seal, label and freeze for up to 2 months.
DEFROSTING/REHEATING DETAILS
Power Setting: Defrost and Full/Maximum
Defrosting and Cooking Time: 26-33 minutes.
1. Remove all wrappings and cook on defrost power for 15 minutes. Leave to stand for 5-10 minutes.
2. If serving cold, sprinkle with Parmesan cheese and serve while still lightly chilled.
3. To reheat, cover and cook on full/maximum power for 6-8 minutes, stirring twice. Sprinkle with Parmesan cheese to serve.

CREAM OF CARROT SOUP

75 g (3 oz) butter
1 onion, peeled and chopped
1 rasher back bacon, rinded and chopped
1 teaspoon salt
1 teaspoon sugar
freshly ground black pepper
450 g (1 lb) peeled carrots, chopped
1 litre (1¾ pints) chicken stock
To garnish:
150 ml (¼ pint) single cream
croûtons

Power Setting: Full/Maximum
Preparation and Cooking Time: 35 minutes

1. Place the butter in a large bowl and cook for 1 minute to melt. Add the onion, bacon, salt, sugar and pepper to taste. Cover and cook for 3 minutes.
2. Stir in the carrots and stock. Cover and cook for 20 minutes.
3. Purée in a blender until smooth or pass through a fine sieve.
4. If serving immediately, turn the soup into a tureen and cook for 2 minutes to reheat. Serve hot, garnished with a swirl of cream and a few croûtons.

FREEZING DETAILS
1. Prepare the recipe to the end of step 3.
2. Cool quickly, transfer to a rigid container, allowing 2.5 cm (1 inch) headspace. Cover, seal, label and freeze for up to 3 months.
REHEATING DETAILS
Power Setting: Full/Maximum
Defrosting and Cooking Time: 14-17 minutes
1. Remove all wrappings and place the frozen soup in a serving tureen. Cook for 14-17 minutes, breaking up the soup and stirring every 3 minutes.
2. Serve hot, garnished with a swirl of cream and a few croûtons.

Variation:
Cream of Artichoke and Carrot Soup: Prepare and cook as above but use 225 g (8 oz) peeled and chopped Jerusalem artichokes and 225 g (8 oz) peeled and chopped carrots instead of all carrots.

SPEEDY STIR-FRIED CHICKEN

350 g (12 oz) boneless chicken breasts, skinned and sliced into thin strips
2 tablespoons dry sherry
1 tablespoon soy sauce
1 teaspoon Chinese 5-spice powder
2 carrots, peeled and cut into thin strips
1 red pepper, cored, seeded and cut into thin strips
1 green pepper, cored, seeded and cut into thin strips
50 g (2 oz) mini corn on the cob
100 g (4 oz) Chinese leaves, thickly shredded
2 canned pineapple slices, chopped
salt
freshly ground black pepper
25 g (1 oz) cashew nuts
To garnish:
sprigs of fresh parsley

Power Setting: Full/Maximum
Preparation and Cooking Time: 15 minutes, plus marinating

1. Place the chicken in a bowl with the sherry, soy sauce and Chinese 5-spice powder, mix well. Cover and leave to marinate for 30 minutes. Meanwhile prepare the other ingredients.
2. Place the carrots and peppers in a bowl. Cover and cook for 2 minutes.
3. Mix the mini corn with the chicken. Cover and cook for 4 minutes, stirring once. Remove the cover and cook for a further 2 minutes.
4. Add the carrot and pepper mixture, Chinese leaves and pineapple pieces, blending well. Add salt and pepper to taste. Cook for 4 minutes, stirring twice. Transfer to a serving dish.
5. To serve immediately, sprinkle with the nuts, garnish with parsley and serve with boiled rice.

FREEZING DETAILS
1. Prepare the recipe to the end of step 4 and transfer to a suitable container.
2. Cool quickly, cover, seal, label and freeze up to 1 month.
REHEATING DETAILS
Power Setting: Defrost and Full/Maximum
Defrosting and Cooking Time: 24 minutes
1. Remove all wrappings and cook on defrost power for 10 minutes, stirring twice. Leave to stand for 10 minutes.
2. Cook on full/maximum power for 4 minutes, stirring twice. Sprinkle with the nuts, garnish with parsley and serve at once with boiled rice.

Bacon ratatouille;
Cream of carrot soup;
Speedy stir-fried chicken

FAMILY MEALS

PUNCHY HOT POT

1 tablespoon oil
675 g (1½ lb) turkey thigh meat, cubed, or turkey casserole
  meat
25 g (1 oz) seasoned flour
1 large onion, peeled and sliced
1 garlic clove, peeled and crushed
100 g (4 oz) carrots, peeled and sliced
200 ml (7 fl oz) brown ale
200 ml (7 fl oz) beef stock
1 teaspoon vinegar
1 teaspoon sugar
1½ teaspoons tomato purée
½ teaspoon Worcestershire sauce
1 bay leaf
salt
100 g (4 oz) button mushrooms, wiped and halved

Power Setting: Full/Maximum and Medium
Preparation and Cooking Time: about 1 hour

1. Place the oil in a large casserole and cook on full/maximum power for 1 minute.
2. Toss the turkey in the flour. Add to the oil with the onion, garlic and carrots, blending well. Cover and cook on full/maximum power for 10 minutes.
3. Add the brown ale, stock, vinegar, sugar, tomato purée. Worcestershire sauce, bay leaf and salt to taste, blending well. Cover and cook on full/maximum power for 10 minutes.
4. Reduce the power setting to medium and cook for 20 minutes, stirring once.
5. Stir in the mushrooms, cover and cook for a further 10 minutes. Remove and discard the bay leaf. Serve with noodles or boiled rice.

FREEZING DETAILS
1. Prepare the recipe to the end of step 5.
2. Cool quickly, cover, seal, label and freeze for up to 3 months.
REHEATING DETAILS
Power Setting: Defrost and Full/Maximum
Defrosting and Cooking Time: 37 minutes
1. Remove all wrappings. Cover and cook on defrost power for 25 minutes, stirring twice.
2. Cook on full/maximum power for 12 minutes, stirring twice.
3. Serve hot with noodles or boiled rice.

LIVER AND BACON CASSEROLE

2 tablespoons oil
2 tablespoons plain flour
½ teaspoon salt
¼ teaspoon freshly ground black pepper
550 g (1¼ lb) lamb's liver, thinly sliced
100 g (4 oz) streaky bacon, rinded and chopped
2 onions, peeled and sliced
1 turnip, peeled and chopped
1 stick celery, scrubbed and chopped
50 g (2 oz) carrots, peeled and chopped
300 ml (½ pint) boiling beef stock
1 tablespoon tomato purée
To garnish:
4 rashers streaky bacon, rinded

Power Setting: Full/Maximum and Medium
Preparation and Cooking Time: About 1¼ hours

1. Blend the oil, flour, salt and pepper in a large casserole. Cook on full/maximum power for 2-3 minutes or until the colour of the mixture is slightly darkened.
2. Add the liver and bacon, tossing well to coat. Cook on full/maximum power for 5 minutes, stirring once.
3. Add the remaining ingredients. Cover and cook on full/maximum power for 10 minutes, stirring once.
4. Reduce the power setting to medium and cook for a further 35 minutes, stirring twice. Leave to stand for 5 minutes.
5. To serve immediately, pleat the 4 bacon rashers and thread on to a wooden skewer or use cocktail sticks. Cook on full/maximum power for 2-3 minutes until crisp, then use as a garnish.

FREEZING DETAILS
1. Prepare the recipe to the end of step 4.
2. Cool quickly, cover, seal, label and freeze for up to 2 months.
REHEATING DETAILS
Power Setting: Defrost and Full/Maximum
Defrosting and Cooking Time: 42-43 minutes
1. Remove all wrappings. Cook the casserole, covered, on defrost power for 25 minutes.
2. Cook on full/maximum power for 12 minutes, stirring twice. Leave to stand for 3 minutes while completing step 5 above.

FROM TOP: Punchy hot pot; Liver and bacon casserole

ROAST CHICKEN WITH WALNUT AND ORANGE STUFFING

1 × 1.75 kg (4 lb) fresh oven-ready chicken
25 g (1 oz) butter
1 tablespoon plain flour
300 ml (½ pint) chicken stock
Stuffing:
50 g (2 oz) butter
1 small onion, peeled and finely chopped
100 g (4 oz) fresh white breadcrumbs
25 g (1 oz) chopped fresh parsley
grated rind of 1 orange and 2 tablespoons orange juice
50 g (2 oz) walnuts, chopped
salt
freshly ground black pepper
1 egg, beaten
To garnish:
orange slices
sprigs of fresh parsley

Power Setting: Full/Maximum
Preparation and Cooking Time: 1 hour

1. To make the stuffing, put the butter in a bowl. Cook for ½-1 minute to melt. Add the onion, cover and cook for 2 minutes.
2. Add the breadcrumbs, three-quarters of the parsley, orange rind and juice, walnuts, and salt and pepper. Add sufficient beaten egg to bind. Use to stuff the neck end of the chicken. Secure with cocktail sticks. Roll the remaining stuffing into balls.
3. To serve immediately, shield the tips of the wings with small pieces of aluminium foil (see note on shielding, page 6). Place on a roasting rack or upturned saucer in a dish and dot with butter.
4. Cook for 26-34 minutes, giving a half-turn halfway through. Cover with aluminium foil and leave to stand for 15 minutes.
5. Meanwhile, place the stuffing balls in a ring on a plate or roasting rack and cook for 2-3 minutes, turning the plate once. Sprinkle with the remaining parsley.
6. To make the gravy, place 2 tablespoons of the chicken juices in a bowl and stir in the flour. Cook for 3 minutes until the flour turns golden. Gradually add the stock, mixing well. Cook for 2-3 minutes, stirring every 1 minute, until smooth and boiling.
7. Garnish the chicken with orange and parsley.

FREEZING DETAILS
1. Prepare the recipe to the end of step 2.
2. Wrap the chicken and stuffing balls separately in aluminium foil. Seal, label and freeze for up to 3 months.
REHEATING DETAILS
Power Setting: Defrost and Full/Maximum
Defrosting and Cooking Time: about 1¼ hours
1. Remove all wrappings. Cook the chicken on defrost power for 26 minutes, turning it occasionally. Leave to stand for 5 minutes.
2. Meanwhile, cook the stuffing balls on defrost power for 5 minutes. Leave to stand while following steps 4-7 above.
3. To make the gravy cook the frozen juices on full/maximum power for 2-3 minutes, stirring once. Continue from Step 6 above.

RABBIT CASSEROLE WITH BACON AND SAGE DUMPLINGS

1 tablespoon oil
675 g (1 ½ lb) boneless rabbit or 4 large rabbit joints
2 tablespoons seasoned flour
1 onion, peeled and sliced
1 garlic clove, peeled and crushed
75 g (3 oz) streaky bacon, rinded and chopped
4 celery sticks, scrubbed and chopped
2 leeks, washed and sliced
2 carrots, peeled and sliced
400 ml (14 fl oz) hot chicken stock
1 bouquet garni
salt
freshly ground black pepper
Dumplings:
25 g (1 oz) streaky bacon, rinded and chopped
50 g (2 oz) self-raising flour
25 g (1 oz) shredded beef suet
1 tablespoon chopped fresh sage or 2 teaspoons dried sage
cold water to mix
To garnish:
celery leaves

Power Setting: Full/Maximum and Medium
Preparation and Cooking Time: about 1 ½ hours

1. Place the oil in a large casserole and cook on full/maximum power for 1 minute.
2. Toss the rabbit in the flour. Add to the oil with the onion, garlic, bacon, celery, leeks and carrots. Cover and cook on full/maximum power for 10 minutes. Add the stock, bouquet garni, salt and pepper. Cover and cook on full/maximum power for 5 minutes.
3. Reduce the power setting to medium and cook for 30 minutes, stirring twice.
4. To serve immediately, place all the dumpling ingredients in a bowl and mix to a soft dough. Turn on to a floured surface and form into 4 dumplings.
5. Stir the casserole and add the dumplings. Cover and cook on medium power for 20 minutes. Allow to stand for 5 minutes. Remove and discard the bouquet garni and garnish with celery leaves.

FREEZING DETAILS
1. Prepare the recipe to the end of step 3.
2. Cool quickly, remove and discard the bouquet garni, cover, seal, label and freeze for up to 3 months.
REHEATING DETAILS
Power Setting: Defrost, Full/Maximum and Medium
Defrosting and Cooking Time: about 1 hour
1. Remove all wrappings. Cover and cook on defrost power for 25 minutes, stirring twice.
2. Cook on full/maximum power for 10 minutes, stirring once.
3. Continue from step 4 above.

Roast chicken with walnut and orange stuffing;
Rabbit casserole with bacon and sage dumplings

SLIPPER PUDDING

Suet Pastry:
215 g (8 oz) self-raising flour
salt
100 g (4oz) shredded beef suet
150 ml (¼ pint) cold water
Filling:
225 g (8 oz) lean cooked bacon, chopped
25 g (1 oz) plain flour
1 teaspoon dried sage
1 onion, peeled and chopped
1 small cooking apple, peeled, cored and grated
100 g (4 oz) button mushrooms, wiped and sliced
freshly ground black pepper
150 ml (¼ pint) chicken stock

Power Setting: Full/Maximum
Preparation and Cooking Time: 30-40 minutes

1. Sift the flour and a pinch of salt into a bowl. Stir in the suet and water and mix quickly, using a round-bladed knife, to form a light elastic dough. Knead lightly until smooth and free from cracks.
2. Roll out the pastry on a lightly floured surface to a round about 5 cm (2 inches) larger than the diameter of a 900 ml (1½ pint) pudding basin. Cut a quarter section from the pastry round and reserve for a lid.
3. Lift the remaining piece of pastry and ease it into the basin, pinching the 2 cut edges together to seal and moulding the pastry on to the base and round the sides of the basin.
4. Toss the bacon in the flour. Add the sage, onion, apple and mushrooms and pepper to taste. Spoon into the basin and pour over the stock.
5. Roll out the remaining pastry to a round large enough to make a lid. Dampen the pastry edges with water and cover with the lid. Pinch the edges together firmly to seal.
6. Cover with cling film, snipping 2 holes in the top to allow the steam to escape. Cook for 12 minutes, giving the dish a quarter-turn every 3 minutes. Allow to stand for 10 minutes. Serve hot with fresh vegetables in season.

FREEZING DETAILS
1. Prepare the recipe to the end of step 6.
2. Cool quickly, wrap in aluminium foil, seal, label and freeze for up to 1 month.
REHEATING DETAILS
Power Setting: Defrost and Full/Maximum
Defrosting and Cooking Time: 21-23 minutes
1. Remove all wrappings. Cook on defrost power for 6 minutes. Leave to stand for 10 minutes.
2. Cover and cook on full/maximum power for 5-7 minutes. Serve hot with fresh vegetables in season.

BEAN LASAGNE

175 g (6 oz) lasagne
1 teaspoon oil
900 ml (1½ pints) boiling water
salt
Beef and bean sauce:
1 tablespoon oil
1 large onion, peeled and chopped
225 g (8 oz) minced beef
1 × 450 g (1 lb) can baked beans in tomato sauce
2 tablespoons tomato purée
½ teaspoon ground nutmeg
freshly ground black pepper
100 g (4 oz) Cheddar cheese, grated

Power Setting: Full/Maximum
Preparation and Cooking Time: 35 minutes

1. Place the lasagne in a deep rectangular casserole. Add the oil, water and a pinch of salt. Cover and cook for 9 minutes. Leave to stand while preparing the sauce, then drain thoroughly.

FROM RIGHT, CLOCKWISE:
Trout with orange;
Bean lasagne; Slipper pudding

2. Place the oil in a bowl with the onion, cover and cook for 3 minutes. Add the beef and cook for 3 minutes, breaking up the beef and stirring twice.

3. Add the beans, tomato purée, nutmeg and salt and pepper to taste, blending well. Cook for 10 minutes, stirring once.

4. Layer the lasagne and beef and bean sauce in the casserole, finishing with a layer of sauce.

5. To serve immediately, sprinkle with the cheese and cook for 2-4 minutes until heated through. Alternatively, place under a preheated grill until golden if wished.

FREEZING DETAILS

1. Prepare the recipe to the end of step 4.

2. Cool quickly, cover, seal, label and freeze for up to 3 months.

REHEATING DETAILS

Power Setting: Defrost and Full/Maximum
Defrosting and Cooking Time: 40-41 minutes

1. Remove all wrappings. Cook on defrost power for 25 minutes. Leave to stand for 10 minutes.

2. Cook on full/maximum power for 3-4 minutes to reheat.

3. Sprinkle with the cheese and cook on full/maximum power for 2 minutes *or* place under a preheated grill until golden.

TROUT WITH ORANGE

4 × 175 g (6 oz) trout, cleaned
Stuffing:
25 g (1 oz) butter
1 small onion, peeled and chopped
50 g (2 oz) mushrooms, wiped and chopped
6 tablespoons fresh white breadcrumbs
2 tablespoons chopped fresh parsley
salt
freshly ground black pepper
1 egg, beaten
Orange sauce:
25 g (1 oz) butter
pinch of caster sugar
1 orange, thinly sliced
8 tablespoons orange juice
1 ½ tablespoons lemon juice
To garnish:
fresh dill or sprigs of parsley

Power Setting: Full/Maximum
Preparation and Cooking Time: 35 minutes

1. Remove the heads from the trout and bone if preferred.

2. Place the butter in a bowl and cook for ½ minute to melt. Add the onion, cover and cook for 2 minutes. Stir in the mushrooms, cover and cook for 1 minute.

3. Stir in the breadcrumbs, parsley and salt and pepper to taste. Bind together with the beaten egg. Use to stuff the trout and place in a shallow oblong dish, top next to tail and stuffing pockets uppermost.

4. Cover and cook for 5 minutes. Turn the dish and cook for 5 minutes. Leave to stand, covered, while preparing the orange sauce.

5. Preheat a small browning dish for 6 minutes (or according to the manufacturer's instructions). Add the butter and sugar and swirl to coat. Add the orange slices and turn quickly on all sides to brown lightly. Add the orange juice and lemon juice and cook for 2 minutes.

6. To serve immediately, garnish with the orange slices and dill or parsley and spoon over the orange sauce.

FREEZING DETAILS

1. Prepare the recipe to the end of step 5.

2. Cool quickly, place in a rigid container, cover, seal, label and freeze for up to 2 months.

REHEATING DETAILS

Power Setting: Defrost and Full/Maximum
Defrosting and Cooking Time: 23-25 minutes

1. Remove all wrappings and place on a shallow oblong dish. Cover and cook on defrost power for 20 minutes.

2. Cook on full/maximum power for 3-5 minutes to reheat. Garnish with the orange slices and dill or parsley. Spoon over the orange sauce.

SWEET AND SOUR MEATBALLS

2 tablespoons oil
1 onion, peeled and finely chopped
450 g (1 lb) lean minced beef
50 g (2 oz) fresh white or brown breadcrumbs
1 teaspoon Worcestershire sauce
salt
freshly ground black pepper
1 egg, beaten
Sauce:
1 tablespoon oil
1 red pepper, cored, seeded and chopped
1 green pepper, cored, seeded and chopped
2 tablespoons soft brown sugar
2 teaspoons soy sauce
2 tablespoons vinegar
120 ml (4 fl oz) orange juice
120 ml (4 fl oz) beef stock
2 teaspoons cornflour
To garnish:
sprigs of fresh parsley

Power Setting: Full/Maximum
Preparation and Cooking Time: 30-35 minutes

1. Heat the oil in a large dish for ½ minute. Add the onion and cook for 3 minutes, stirring once.
2. Meanwhile, mix the beef, breadcrumbs, Worcestershire sauce, salt and pepper to taste and enough egg to bind the mixture.
3. Divide into 8 portions and roll into balls. Place these in a single layer on top of the onion. Cook for 5 minutes, turning once. Leave to stand while preparing the sauce.
4. Place the oil and peppers in a bowl. Cover and cook for 4 minutes, stirring once. Stir in the sugar, soy sauce, vinegar, orange juice, beef stock and cornflour, blending well. Cook for 3 mintues, stirring every 1 minute.
5. Pour over the meatballs and cook for 5 minutes. Garnish with parsley and serve with boiled rice or jacket potatoes.

FREEZING DETAILS
1. Prepare the recipe to the end of step 5.
2. Cool quickly, cover, seal, label and freeze for up to 3 months.
REHEATING DETAILS
Power Setting: Defrost and Full/Maximum
Defrosting and Cooking Time: 31-35 mintues
1. Remove all wrappings. Cook on defrost power for 8-10 minutes. Leave to stand for 15 minutes.
2. Cook on full/maximum power for 8-10 minutes, turning once. Garnish with parsley and serve with boiled rice or jacket potatoes.

Pork spareribs provençal;
Sweet and sour meatballs

PORK SPARERIBS PROVENÇAL

Serves 6
6 pork sparerib chops
Marinade:
6 tablespoons oil
3 tablespoons white wine vinegar
1 tablespoon chopped fresh parsley
2 garlic cloves, peeled and crushed
Provençal sauce:
1 tablespoon oil
1 onion, peeled and finely chopped
1 green pepper, cored, seeded and chopped
1 tablespoon tomato purée
1 × 400 g (14 oz) can peeled tomatoes
1 teaspoon sugar
1 teaspoon Worcestershire sauce
2 teaspoons cornflour
salt
freshly ground black pepper
To garnish:
sprigs of fresh parsley

Power Setting: Full/Maximum and Medium
Preparation and Cooking Time: about 50 minutes, plus marinating

1. Place the chops in a shallow dish.
2. Mix the oil with the vinegar, parsley and garlic, blending well. Pour over the chops and leave to marinate for 4 hours.
3. To cook, preheat a large browning dish on full/maximum power for 8 minutes (or according to the manufacturer's instructions).
4. Add the pork chops and turn quickly on all sides to brown evenly. Cook on medium power for 26 minutes. Remove, cover with aluminium foil and leave to stand while preparing the sauce.
5. Place the oil in a bowl and cook on full/maximum power for 1 minute. Add the onion and pepper, cover and cook on full/maximum power for 4 minutes. Stir in the tomato purée, chopped tomatoes with their juice, sugar, Worcestershire sauce and cornflour dissolved in a little cold water. Add salt and pepper to taste and cook the provençal sauce on full/maximum power for 6 minutes, stirring twice.
6. Garnish with parsley and serve the chops with the sauce.

FREEZING DETAILS
1. Prepare the recipe to the end of step 5.
2. Cool quickly, place the chops and sauce in a rigid freezer container. Cover, seal, label and freeze for up to 3 months.
REHEATING DETAILS
Power Setting: Defrost and Full/Maximum
Defrosting and Cooking Time: 38-40 mintues
1. Remove all wrappings. Place the frozen pork mixture in a serving dish and cook on defrost power for 25 minutes. Allow to stand for 5 minutes.
2. Cook on full/maximum power for 8-10 minutes.
3. Garnish with parsley.

FARMHOUSE ORCHARD SCONES

Makes 8
175 g (6 oz) plain wholewheat flour
50 g (2 oz) plain flour
½ teaspoon salt
4 teaspoons baking powder
50 g (2 oz) butter
1 egg, beaten
about 4-6 tablespoons milk
cracked wheat to sprinkle (optional)

Filling:
2 red-skinned apples
2 tablespoons lemon juice
100-175 g (4-6 oz) full fat soft cheese

Power Setting: Full/Maximum
Preparation and Cooking Time: 20-25 minutes

1. Sift the flours, salt and baking powder into a bowl. Rub in the butter until the mixture resembles fine breadcrumbs.
2. Stir in the egg and sufficient milk to form a soft dough. Knead on a lightly floured surface until smooth.
3. Grease an 18 cm (7 inch) flan dish and line the base with lightly greased greaseproof paper. Shape the dough into an 18 cm (7 inch) round and place in the dish. Mark into 8 wedges with a sharp knife. Sprinkle the top with cracked wheat (if used).
4. Cook for 2 minutes, give the dish a half-turn and cook for a further 2-2¼ minutes.
5. Allow to cool slightly before turning on to a wire tray to cool.
6. To serve immediately, core both apples and cut one into 8 thick slices. Toss in half of the lemon juice. Finely chop the remaining apple and toss in the remaining lemon juice. Fold the chopped apple into the cheese, blending well.
7. Break the scones in half, fill with the cheese mixture and with the apple slices.

FREEZING DETAILS
1. Prepare the recipe to the end of step 5.
2. Cool quickly, wrap in aluminium foil, seal, label and freeze for up to 3 months.

DEFROSTING DETAILS
Power Setting: Defrost
Defrosting Time: 3-3½ minutes
1. Remove all wrappings. Place on a sheet of paper towel and cook for 3-3½ minutes.
2. Continue from step 6 above.

STRAWBERRY AND GRAND MARNIER PRESERVE

Makes about 1.5 kg (3½ lb)
550 g (1¼ lb) strawberries, hulled
900 g (2 lb) caster sugar
2-3 tablespoons Grand Marnier
½ bottle liquid pectin
2 tablespoons lemon juice

Power Setting: Full/Maximum
Preparation and Cooking Time: 1¼ hours, plus standing

1. Crush the strawberries with the sugar and Grand Marnier in a bowl. Cook for 1 minute. Stir well and leave the mixture to stand for 30 minutes.
2. Stir and cook for ½ minute. Leave to stand for a further 30

Farmhouse orchard scones;
Strawberry and Grand Marnier
preserve; Chocolate biscuits

minutes.

3. Add the pectin and lemon juice, blending well.

4. Pour into 3-4 small freezerproof jars, leaving 1 cm (½ inch) headspace. Cover with aluminium foil and leave to stand in a warm kitchen for 48 hours.

5. Alternatively, some of the preserve may now be served with scones, teabreads, or as a sponge cake filling. Store in the refrigerator for up to 1 week.

FREEZING DETAILS
1. Prepare the recipe to the end of step 4.
2. Seal and label the jars and freeze for up to 6 months.
DEFROSTING DETAILS
Power Setting: Full/Maximum
Defrosting Time: 17-18 minutes
1. Remove the aluminium foil lid and cook each jar for 2-3 minutes. Leave to stand for 15 minutes, stirring twice.
2. Serve with scones, teabreads, or as a sponge cake filling.

CHOCOLATE BISCUITS

Makes 24
225 g (8 oz) butter
100 g (4 oz) muscovado sugar
1 teaspoon vanilla essence
225 g (8 oz) self-raising flour
50 g (2 oz) powdered chocolate

Power Setting: Full/Maximum
Preparation and Cooking Time: 25 minutes

1. Cream the butter with the sugar and vanilla essence until light and fluffy.
2. Sift the flour with the chocolate and gradually add to the butter mixture to make a smooth dough.
3. Form teaspoons of the mixture into 24 small balls about the size of a walnut. Flatten each ball with a fork.
4. Place 6 at a time on a microwave baking tray or lightly greased greaseproof paper and cook for 1¾-2¼ minutes, depending upon size. Give the tray or paper a half-turn halfway through the cooking time. Allow to cool on a wire tray. Repeat with the remaining mixture.

FREEZING DETAILS
1. Prepare the recipe to the end of step 4.
2. Cool quickly, place in a rigid freezer box, interleaved with freezer film, cover, seal, label and freeze for up to 6 months.
DEFROSTING DETAILS
Power Setting: Full/Maximum
Defrosting Time: 11 minutes
1. Remove all wrappings and place the biscuits on a plate. Cook for 1 minute. Leave to stand for 10 minutes before serving.

Variation: Chocolate Chip Biscuits: Prepare and cook the biscuits as above but use 50 g/2 oz chocolate polka dots instead of powdered chocolate.

SULTANA SQUARES

Makes 8:
225 g (8 oz) self-raising flour
pinch of salt.
100 g (4 oz) butter
100 g (4 oz) light muscovado or soft brown sugar
¼ teaspoon ground cinnamon
150 g (5 oz) sultanas
2 eggs, beaten
about 4-6 tablespoons milk

Power Setting: Full/Maximum
Preparation and Cooking Time: 15 minutes

1. Lightly grease an 18 cm (7 inch) square cake dish and line the base with lightly greased greaseproof paper.
2. Sift the flour and salt into a bowl. Rub in the butter until the mixture resembles fine breadcrumbs.
3. Stir in the sugar, cinnamon and sultanas, blending well. Add the eggs and sufficient milk to make a soft dropping consistency.
4. Spoon into the prepared dish and cook for 5½-7 minutes, giving the dish a quarter-turn every 1½ minutes. Allow to cool slightly before turning out on a wire tray. Cut into 8 squares.

FREEZING DETAILS
1. Prepare the recipe to the end of step 4.
2. Cool quickly, place in a rigid freezer box, cover, seal, label and freeze for up to 6 months.
DEFROSTING DETAILS
Power Setting: Defrost
Defrosting Time: 8 minutes
1. Remove all wrappings and place on paper towels. Cook for 3 minutes. Leave to stand for 5 minutes, to cool. Cut into 8 squares.

Sultana squares; Spicy currant biscuits; Gingered walnut flan

GINGERED WALNUT FLAN

Pastry:
225 g (8 oz) plain flour
pinch of salt
50 g (2 oz) lard
50 g (2 oz) butter
1 tablespoon caster sugar
2-3 tablespoons iced water

Filling:
50 g (2 oz) butter
3 eggs, beaten
175 g (6 oz) soft dark brown sugar
1 teaspoon ground ginger
5 tablespoons golden syrup
175 g (6 oz) walnuts, coarsely chopped
whipped cream, to serve

Power Setting: Full/Maximum and Medium
Preparation and Cooking Time: about 1 hour

1. Sift the flour with the salt into a bowl. Rub in the lard and butter until the mixture resembles fine breadcrumbs. Stir in the sugar and water and bind together to a firm but pliable dough. Turn on to a lightly floured surface and knead until smooth and crackfree.
2. Roll out the pastry on a lightly floured surface to a round large enough to line a 23 cm (9 inch) flan dish. Press in firmly, taking care not to stretch the pastry. Cut the pastry away, leaving a 5 mm (¼ inch) 'collar' above the dish to allow for any shrinkage that may occur (see right). Prick the base and sides well with a fork.
3. Place a double thickness of paper towels over the base, easing into position around the edges.
4. Cook on full/maximum power for 3½ minutes, giving the dish a quarter-turn every 1 minute. Remove the paper and cook on full/maximum power for a further 1½ minutes.
5. Prepare the filling by placing the butter in a bowl. Cook on full/maximum power for ¾-1 minute to melt. Stir in the eggs, sugar, ginger, syrup and walnuts, blending well.
6. Spoon into the flan case and cook on medium power for 18-20 minutes, giving the dish a quarter-turn every 4½ minutes, until set. Allow to cool.
7. Serve cut into wedges topped with swirls of whipped cream.

FREEZING DETAILS
1. Prepare the recipe to the end of step 6.
2. Cool quickly, cover with aluminium foil, seal, label and freeze for up to 3 months.
DEFROSTING DETAILS
Power Setting: Full/Maximum
Defrosting Time: 10 minutes
1. Remove all wrappings. Cook on full/maximum power for 5 minutes, turning once. Allow to stand for 5 minutes.
2. Serve cut into wedges, topped with swirls of whipped cream.

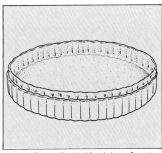
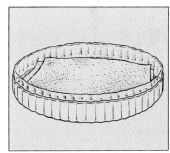
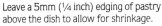

Leave a 5mm (¼ inch) edging of pastry above the dish to allow for shrinkage.

Place a double thickness of paper towel over the base.

SPICY CURRANT BISCUITS

Makes 30
225 g (8 oz) plain flour
½ teaspoon ground mixed spice
¼ teaspoon ground nutmeg
175 g (6 oz) butter, softened
75 g (3 oz) currants
150 g (5 oz) demerara sugar

Power Setting: Full/Maximum
Preparation and Cooking Time: 25 minutes

1. Sift the flour with the mixed spice and nutmeg. Add the butter, currants and 100 g (4 oz) of the demerara sugar. Knead to make a firm dough.
2. Divide the mixture into 2 pieces and form each into a 15 cm (6 inch) long roll. Roll in the remaining sugar to coat.
3. Using a sharp knife, cut each roll into 15 slices. Place 6 at a time on a microwave baking sheet or lightly greased greaseproof paper and cook for 1¾-2¼ minutes. Give the baking sheet or paper a half-turn halfway through the cooking time. Allow to cool on a wire tray. Repeat with the remaining mixture.

FREEZING DETAILS
1. Prepare the recipe to the end of step 3.
2. Cool quickly, place in a rigid freezer box, interleaved with freezer film. Cover, seal, label and freeze for up to 6 months.
DEFROSTING DETAILS
Power Setting: Full/Maximum
Defrosting Time: 11 minutes
1. Remove all wrappings and place the biscuits on a plate. Cook for 1 minute. Leave to stand for 10 minutes before serving.

GOOSEBERRY AND MINT PUDDING

Sponge pudding:
100 g (4 oz) butter
100 g (4 oz) caster sugar
2 eggs, beaten
100 g (4 oz) self-raising flour
pinch of salt
1-2 tablespoons hot water
4-5 tablespoons gooseberry jam
½ teaspoon chopped fresh mint

Custard:
300 ml (½ pint) milk
2 eggs
1 tablespoon caster sugar
1 teaspoon cornflour
2-3 drops vanilla essence

Power Setting: Full/Maximum
Preparation and Cooking Time: 40 minutes

1. Line a 900 ml (1 ½ pint) pudding basin with cling film or grease the basin well.
2. Cream the butter with the sugar until light and fluffy. Add the eggs, blending well. Sift the flour with the salt and fold into the mixture with a metal spoon. Add enough water to make a soft dropping consistency.
3. Mix the jam with the mint and place in the bottom of the prepared basin. Spoon the sponge mixture on top. Cover with cling film, snipping 2 holes in the top to allow the steam to escape. Cook for 6-7 minutes, turning the basin once. Leave to stand for 5-10 minutes.
4. To serve immediately, place the milk in a jug and cook for about 3 minutes or until almost boiling. Lightly beat the eggs, sugar, cornflour and vanilla essence together. Pour the milk on to this mixture, stir well to blend and strain back into the jug.
5. Return to the oven in a deep dish containing hand-hot water to come halfway up the sides and cook for 4 minutes, stirring every 1 minute to keep the sauce smooth. The custard is cooked when it lightly coats the back of the spoon. Serve with the turned out sponge pudding.

FREEZING DETAILS

1. Prepare the recipe to the end of step 3.
2. Cover, seal, label and freeze for up to 3 months.
REHEATING DETAILS
Power Setting: Defrost and Full/Maximum
Defrosting and Cooking Time: 13-14 minutes
1. Remove all wrappings. Cook on defrost power for 1½-2 minutes. Allow to stand for 10 minutes.
2. Cover and cook on full/maximum power for 1½-2 minutes. Leave to stand while preparing the custard from step 4 above.

MOCHA HONEY GÂTEAU

Cake:
175 g (6 oz) butter
75 g (3 oz) demerara sugar
2 tablespoons clear honey
3 eggs, beaten
120 g (4½ oz) self-raising flour
40 g (1 ½ oz) cocoa powder
1 teaspoon instant coffee granules
4 tablespoons hot water
few drops of vanilla essence

Filling and topping:
40 g (1 ½ oz) cornflour
450 ml (¾ pint) milk
2 tablespoons instant coffee granules
215 g (7½ oz) light soft brown sugar
350 g (12 oz) butter
65 g (2½ oz) walnuts, finely chopped

To decorate:
chocolate curls or crumbled chocolate flake

Power Setting: Full/Maximum
Preparation and Cooking Time: about 1 hour

1. Line a 20 cm (8 inch) cake dish or soufflé dish with cling film or lightly grease the dish and line the base with lightly greased greaseproof paper.

2. Cream the butter with the sugar and honey until light and fluffy. Add the eggs, one at a time, beating well.

3. Sift the flour with the cocoa powder and fold into the butter mixture with a metal spoon.

4. Dissolve the coffee in the water and stir in the vanilla essence. Fold into the cake mixture with a metal spoon. Spoon into the prepared dish and cook for 5½-6½ minutes, giving the dish a quarter turn every 1½ minutes. Leave to stand for 5-10 minutes before turning out on to a wire tray to cool.

5. To serve immediately, when cold carefully cut the cake horizontally into 3 equal layers.

6. Make the filling and topping by blending the cornflour with a little of the milk in a bowl to form a smooth paste. Place the remaining milk in a jug with the coffee and sugar, cook for 1½ minutes. Add the blended cornflour, stirring well to mix. Cook for 5-6 minutes, stirring twice, until smooth and thick. Cover the surface with greaseproof paper dampened on the top side and leave to cool completely.

7. Beat the butter until creamy. Gradually add the cold coffee sauce, beating well to form a smooth mixture.

8. Mix one-third of the coffee filling with 25 g (1 oz) of the walnuts. Sandwich the cake layers together with this filling. Spread the top and sides of the cake with about half of the remaining coffee mixture. Press the remaining walnuts on to the sides of the cake.

9. Place the remaining coffee mixture in a piping bag fitted with a large star nozzle and pipe swirls on top of the cake.

10. Decorate with chocolate curls or crumbled chocolate flake. Cut into wedges to serve.

FREEZING DETAILS

1. Prepare the recipe to the end of step 4.

2. Place the undecorated cake in a rigid box. Cover, seal, label and freeze for up to 6 months.

DEFROSTING DETAILS

Power Setting: Defrost
Defrosting Time: 8 minutes

1. Remove all wrappings and place on plate. Cook on defrost power for 3 minutes. Leave to stand for 5 minutes.

2. To fill and decorate the cake continue from step 5 above.

Gooseberry and mint pudding; Mocha honey gâteau

HONEY CRUNCH CRUMBLE

675 g (1 ½ lb) cooking apples, peeled, cored and sliced
6 tablespoons clear honey
75 g (3 oz) butter
175 g (6 oz) muesli-style breakfast cereal

Power Setting: Full/Maximum
Preparation and Cooking Time: 25 minutes

1. Put the apples in a serving dish and drizzle over half the honey.
2. Place the butter in a bowl and cook for 1 ½-2 minutes to melt.
3. Stir in the remaining honey and the cereal, mixing well to coat. Spoon on top of the apples. Cook for 11-13 minutes, giving the dish a quarter turn every 3 minutes.
4. Serve hot with cream or custard (see Gooseberry and mint pudding page 38).

FREEZING DETAILS
1. Prepare the recipe to the end of step 3.
2. Cool quickly, cover, seal, label and freeze for up to 3 months.
REHEATING DETAILS
Power Setting: Full/Maximum
Defrosting and Reheating Time: 12-13 minutes
1. Remove all wrappings. Cook for 5 minutes, turning the dish once. Allow to stand for 5 minutes.
2. Cook for a further 2-3 minutes. Serve hot with cream or custard (see Gooseberry and mint pudding page 38).

BLACK CHERRY CREAM PIE

Base:
100 g (4 oz) butter
165 g (5½ oz) bran flakes
1 ½ tablespoons soft brown sugar
Filling:
1 × 425 g (15 oz) can black cherries in syrup
1 × 135 g (4¾ oz) packet black cherry jelly tablet
300 ml (½ pint) black cherry yogurt
300 ml (½ pint) double cream, whipped

Power Setting: Full/Maximum
Preparation and Cooking Time: 15 minutes, plus chilling

1. Place the butter in a large bowl and cook for 1 ½-2 minutes to melt. Stir in the bran flakes and sugar, tossing well to coat. Press on to the base and sides of a deep 23 cm (9 inch) flan tin with a removable base. Chill to set, for about 30 minutes.
2. Drain the juice from the cherries into a bowl. Add the jelly and cook for 2½-3½ minutes, stirring once to dissolve completely. Chill until just beginning to set.
3. Whisk the jelly with the yogurt until foamy. Fold in half the

TOP TO BOTTOM: Honey crunch crumble;
Black cherry cream pie; Winter pudding

cream with a metal spoon. Pour into the pie case. Chill to set.
4. Pipe or swirl the remaining cream on top of the pie and decorate with the black cherries. Serve chilled.

FREEZING DETAILS
1. Prepare the recipe to the end of step 3.
2. Place in a rigid container, cover, seal, label and freeze for up to 3 months.
DEFROSTING DETAILS
Power Setting: Defrost
Defrosting Time: 1-2 hours
1. Remove all wrappings. This dessert is best defrosted at room temperature for 6 hours. To speed up this time, however, cook on defrost power for 1 minute. Leave to stand for 1 hour.

WINTER PUDDING

75 g (3 oz) self-raising flour
pinch of salt
½ teaspoon ground mixed spice
75 g (3 oz) fresh wholemeal breadcrumbs
75 g (3 oz) shredded beef suet
50 g (2 oz) soft light brown sugar
50 g (2 oz) sultanas
50 g (2 oz) raisins
50 g (2 oz) currants
grated rind of ½ lemon
about 6 tablespoons milk

Power Setting: Full/Maximum
Preparation and Cooking Time: 20 minutes

1. Sift the flour with the salt and mixed spice. Stir in the breadcrumbs, suet, sugar, sultanas, raisins, currants and lemon rind, blending well. Add sufficient milk to make a soft dropping consistency.
2. Spoon into a greased 900 ml (1 ½ pint) pudding basin and cover with cling film. Snip 2 holes in the top for steam to escape.
3. Cook for 5 minutes, giving the dish a half-turn twice.
4. Leave to stand for 5 minutes before turning out on to a warmed serving plate. Serve with custard (see Gooseberry and mint pudding page 38).

FREEZING DETAILS
1. Prepare the recipe to the end of step 3.
2. Cool quickly, cover the basin with aluminium foil, seal, label and freeze for up to 1 month.
REHEATING DETAILS
Power Setting: Full/Maximum
Defrosting and Cooking Time: 13½-14 minutes
1. Remove all wrappings. Cook on defrost power for 2 minutes. Leave to stand for 10 minutes.
2. Cook on full/maximum power for 1 ½-2 minutes to reheat. Serve with custard (see Gooseberry and mint pudding page 38).

VEGETABLE DISHES

CURRIED BLACK-EYE BEANS

350 g (12 oz) dried black-eye beans
1.5 litres (2½ pints) cold chicken stock
25 g (1 oz) butter
2 carrots, peeled and cut into thin strips
1 onion, peeled and finely chopped
1 celery stick, scrubbed and finely chopped
2-3 teaspoons curry powder
2 tablespoon plain flour
4 tablespoons tomato purée
300 ml (½ pint) beef stock
2 tablespoons Worcestershire sauce
50 g (2 oz) sultanas
salt
freshly ground black pepper

Power Setting: Full/Maximum and Medium
Preparation and Cooking Time: 1 hour 40 minutes

1. Place the beans in a large casserole with the cold chicken stock. Cover and cook on full/maximum power for 20 minutes.
2. Stir, re-cover and cook on medium power for 45-60 minutes until tender, stirring occasionally. Drain thoroughly.
3. Place the butter in a bowl and cook on full power for ½ minute to melt. Add the carrots, onion and celery, blending well. Cover and cook on full/maximum power for 4 minutes, stirring once.
4. Stir in the curry powder and cook for 1 minute. Blend in the flour. Gradually add the tomato purée, beef stock, Worcestershire sauce, sultananas, salt and pepper to taste. Cook on full/maximum power for 5-7 minutes, stirring every 2 minutes until thickened.
5. Stir in the beans. To serve immediately, cook on full/maximum power for 1-2 minutes. Serve with an Indian meal.

FREEZING DETAILS
1. Prepare the recipe to the end of step 4 and stir in the beans.
2. Cool quickly, spoon into a rigid container. Cover, seal, label and freeze for up to 3 months.
REHEATING DETAILS
Power Setting: Defrost and Full/Maximum
Defrosting and Cooking Time: 35-40 minutes
1. Remove all wrappings. Place the frozen bean mixture in a bowl. Cover and cook on defrost power for 25-30 minutes, breaking up the beans and stirring twice. Leave to stand for 5 minutes.
2. Cook on full/maximum power for 5 minutes, stirring once.

VEGETABLE AND CASHEW RICE

50 g (2 oz) butter
1 onion, peeled and chopped
1 garlic clove, peeled and crushed
225 g (8 oz) long-grain brown rice
600 ml (1 pint) boiling water
½ teaspoon ground turmeric
1 teaspoon sea salt
1 large carrot, peeled and cut into thin strips
225 g (8 oz) French beans, cut into 5 cm (2 inch) pieces
1 small red pepper, cored, seeded and chopped
3 tablespoons water
4 tomatoes, peeled and quartered
freshly ground black pepper
175 g (6 oz) toasted cashew nuts

Power Setting: Full/Maximum
Preparation and Cooking Time: about 45 minutes

1. Place the butter in a large casserole and cook for 1 minute to melt. Add the onion, garlic, rice, water, turmeric and salt, blending well. Cover and cook for 20-25 minutes until tender. Leave to stand for 5 minutes, then drain thoroughly if necessary.
2. Meanwhile, place the carrot, beans and red pepper in a bowl with the cold water. Cover and cook for 4-5 minutes, until tender.
3. Drain the vegetables, then fold into the rice mixture with the tomatoes, pepper to taste and half the cashew nuts.
4. To serve immediately, cook for 2-3 minutes to reheat. Serve sprinkled with the remaining cashew nuts.

FREEZING DETAILS
1. Prepare the recipe to the end of step 3.
2. Cool quickly, spoon into a rigid container. Cover, seal, label and freeze for up to 2 months.
REHEATING DETAILS
Power Setting: Defrost and Full/Maximum
Defrosting and Cooking Time: 23-27 minutes
1. Remove all wrappings and place the frozen rice mixture in a bowl. Cook on defrost power for 8-10 minutes, breaking up the rice with a fork every 3 minutes. Leave to stand for 10 minutes.
2. Cook on full/maximum power for 5-7 minutes, stirring once. Serve sprinkled with the remaining cashew nuts.

Curried black-eye beans; Vegetable and cashew rice

CRUMBLY BUTTERED BRUSSELS

450 g (1 lb) Brussels sprouts, trimmed
4 tablespoons water
salt
75 g (3 oz) butter
1 garlic clove, peeled and crushed (optional)
6 tablespoons toasted breadcrumbs
pinch of cayenne pepper

Power Setting: Full/Maximum
Preparation and Cooking Time: 25 minutes

1. Place the sprouts in a dish with the water and a pinch of salt. Cover and cook for 7-9 minutes, stirring once. Drain thoroughly.
2. To serve immediately, place the butter in a bowl and cook for 1½ minutes to melt. Add the garlic (if used) breadcrumbs, salt and cayenne pepper to taste, mixing well. Toss the cooked sprouts in the buttered crumbs. Cook, uncovered, for 3 minutes, stirring once. Serve hot.

FREEZING DETAILS
1. Prepare the recipe to the end of step 1.
2. Place the cooked sprouts in a rigid freezer container, cool quickly, cover, seal, label and freeze for up to 1 month.
REHEATING DETAILS
Power Setting: Full/Maximum
Defrosting and Cooking Time: 10½-12½ minutes
1. Remove all wrappings. Place the frozen sprouts in a bowl with 2 tablespoons water. Cover and cook for 6-8 minutes until thawed and warm. Drain thoroughly.
2. To finish, continue with step 2 above.

ORANGE GLAZED CARROTS

450 g (1 lb) carrots, peeled
8 tablespoons fresh orange juice
25 g (1 oz) butter
1 teaspoon brown sugar
finely grated rind of ½ small orange
salt
freshly ground black pepper
To garnish:
chopped fresh parsley

Power Setting: Full/Maximum
Preparation and Cooking Time: 20 minutes

1. Cut the carrots into strips about 1.5 cm (½ inch) wide. Place in a dish with the orange juice. Cover and cook for 10-12 minutes,

RED CABBAGE CASSEROLE

Serves 6
1 medium red cabbage, weighing about 900 g (2 lb), cored and shredded
3 tablespoons apple juice or water
4 cooking apples, peeled, cored and finely chopped
pinch of ground cloves
1 tablespoon white wine vinegar
1 tablespoon brown sugar
1 tablespoon redcurrant jelly
25 g (1 oz) butter

Power Setting: Full/Maximum
Preparation and Cooking Time: 30 minutes

1. Place the red cabbage in a casserole with the apple juice or water and apples. Cover and cook for 12-14 minutes until tender, stirring once.
2. Stir in the cloves, vinegar, sugar, redcurrant jelly and butter, blending well. Cover and cook for 2 minutes.
3. Serve hot with roasts, game, frankfurters or sausages.

FREEZING DETAILS
1. Prepare the recipe to the end of step 2.
2. Cool quickly, spoon into a rigid container, cover, seal, label and freeze for up to 3 months.
REHEATING DETAILS
Power Setting: Full/Maximum
Defrosting and Cooking Time: 12 minutes
1. Remove all wrappings. Place the frozen red cabbage mixture in a serving dish. Cover and cook for 12 minutes, stirring once.

stirring once. Drain thoroughly.
2. Place the butter in a bowl and cook for ½ minute to melt. Stir in the sugar, orange rind and salt and pepper to taste, blending well.
3. Pour over the carrots and toss well to blend. Cover and cook for a further 2 minutes. Serve hot, sprinkled with parsley.

FREEZING DETAILS
1. Prepare the recipe to the end of step 3.
2. Cool quickly, place in a rigid container, cover, seal, label and freeze for up to 3 months.
REHEATING DETAILS
Power Setting: Full/Maximum
Defrosting and Cooking Time: 5-6 minutes
1. Remove all wrappings. Place the frozen carrot mixture in a serving dish with 1 tablespoon water or orange juice. Cover and cook for 5-6 minutes, stirring twice. Serve hot, sprinkled with parsley.

Crumbly buttered Brussels; Red cabbage casserole;
Lemon and garlic potatoes

LEMON AND GARLIC POTATOES

20 g (¾ oz) butter
20 g (¾ oz) plain flour
400 ml (14 fl oz) milk
2 tablespoons lemon juice
grated rind of ½ lemon
1 garlic clove, peeled and crushed
salt
freshly ground black pepper
900 g (2 lb) potatoes, peeled and thinly sliced
To garnish:
chopped chives

Power Setting: Full/Maximum
Preparation and Cooking Time: 35-40 minutes

1. Place the butter in a jug and cook for ½ minute to melt. Add the flour, blending well. Gradually add the milk and cook for 3-4 minutes, stirring every 1 minute until smooth and thickened.
2. Stir in the lemon juice and rind, garlic, salt and pepper.
3. Place half the potato slices in a greased shallow dish. Pour over half the sauce. Top with the remaining potato slices and cover with the remaining sauce.
4. Cover with cling film, snipping 2 holes in the top to allow the steam to escape. Cook for 16 minutes, turning the dish twice. Allow to stand for 5 minutes.
5. To serve immediately, cook under a preheated hot grill until golden if wished. Garnish with chopped chives. Serve hot with chops, steak or chicken.

FREEZING DETAILS
1. Prepare the recipe to the end of step 4.
2. Cool quickly, cover, seal, label and freeze for up to 3 months.
REHEATING DETAILS
Power Setting: Defrost and Full/Maximum
Defrosting and Cooking Time: 26-28 minutes
1. Remove all wrappings. Cover and cook on defrost power for 12 minutes. Allow to stand for 10 minutes.
2. Cook on full/maximum power for 4-6 minutes.
3. To finish, continue with step 5 above.

Variation:
Rosemary and Lemon Potatoes: Prepare and cook as above but use 2 teaspoons chopped fresh rosemary instead of the garlic.

CELERY WITH LEMON AND ALMONDS

25 g (1 oz) butter
350 g (12 oz) celery, scrubbed and cut into 7.5 cm (3 inch)
  lengths
200 ml (7 fl oz) chicken stock or water
100 ml (3½ fl oz) lemon juice
1 tablespoon sugar
salt
freshly ground black pepper
50 g (2 oz) flaked almonds
grated rind of 1 small lemon
To garnish:
celery leaves

Power Setting: Full/Maximum
Preparation and Cooking Time: 30 minutes

1. Place the butter in a shallow dish and cook for ½ minute to melt. Add the celery, tossing well to coat. Cook, uncovered, for 3 minutes.

2. Add the stock or water, lemon juice, sugar and salt and pepper to taste. Cover and cook for 16-18 minutes, turning the dish twice.
3. To serve immediately, leave the celery to stand while preparing the almonds. Place the almonds on a plate and cook for 4-5 minutes, stirring every 1 minute until golden.
4. Serve the celery sprinkled with the lemon rind and toasted almonds. Garnish with celery leaves.

FREEZING DETAILS
1. Prepare the recipe to the end of step 2.
2. Cool quickly, cover, seal, label and freeze for up to 3 months.
REHEATING DETAILS
Power Setting: Full/Maximum
Defrosting and Cooking Time: 12-14 minutes
1. Remove all wrappings, cover and cook on full/maximum power for 3-4 minutes, turning the dish twice. Leave to stand for 5 minutes.
2. Meanwhile, toast the almonds as in step 3 above.
3. Serve the celery sprinkled with the lemon rind and toasted almonds. Garnish with celery leaves.

SPINACH TERRINE

Serves 6-8
20 large fresh spinach leaves
450 g (1 lb) full fat soft cheese
3 egg yolks
100 g (4 oz) cooked ham, minced or finely chopped
2 teaspoons lemon juice
salt
freshly ground black pepper

Power Setting: Full/Maximum and Medium
Preparation and Cooking Time: 25 minutes

1. Wash the spinach leaves well, shake thoroughly and place in a bowl. Cover and cook on full/maximum power for 1 ½ minutes. Drain and rinse under cold running water.
2. Use about 8 of the spinach leaves to line a 20 cm (8 inch) microwave loaf dish.
3. Mix the cheese with egg yolks, ham, lemon juice and salt and pepper to taste.
4. Spoon one-third of the ham mixture into the base of the dish and cover with 4 of the spinach leaves. Repeat twice, finishing with a layer of spinach leaves.
5. Cover with cling film, snipping 2 holes in the top to allow the steam to escape. Cook on medium power for 5 minutes.
6. Give the dish a half-turn and cook on full/maxiumum power for 3-4 minutes or until just set. Allow to cool in the dish.
7. To serve immediately, chill lightly and serve in thin slices with a tomato sauce such as provençal sauce (see Pork spareribs provençal page 33). Serve with crusty bread.

FREEZING DETAILS
1. Prepare the recipe to the end of step 6.
2. Cool quickly in the dish. Cover with aluminium foil, seal, label and freeze for up to 3 months.
REHEATING DETAILS
Power Setting: Defrost
Defrosting Time: 40-50 minutes
1. Remove all wrappings. Cook on defrost power for 20 minutes.
2. Leave to stand for 20-30 minutes before serving, cut into thin slices, with a tomato sauce (see above).

VEGETABLE RISSOLES

100 g (4 oz) red lentils
600 ml (1 pint) boiling chicken stock
1 large onion, peeled and finely chopped
1 celery stick, scrubbed and finely chopped
2 small carrots, peeled and grated
50 g (2 oz) cooked green beans, finely chopped
50 g (2 oz) fresh white breadcrumbs
3 eggs, beaten
1 teaspoon dried mixed herbs
salt
freshly ground black pepper
75 g (3 oz) dry white breadcrumbs
2-3 tablespoons oil

Power Setting: Full/Maximum
Preparation and Cooking Time: about 40 minutes, plus standing

1. Place the lentils and stock in a bowl. Cover and cook for 20 minutes, stirring once. Drain if necessary.
2. Mix the lentils with the onion, celery, carrots, beans, fresh breadcrumbs, 2 of the eggs, herbs and salt and pepper to taste. Leave to stand for 30 minutes.
3. Shape the mixture into 8 rissoles. Dip each of these in the remaining beaten egg and then in the dry breadcrumbs to coat.
4. To serve immediately, preheat a large browning dish for 8 minutes (or according to the manufacturer's instructions). Brush with the oil and cook for a further 1 minute.
5. Add the rissoles and allow to brown on the underside, about 2-3 minutes. Turn over and cook for 4-5 minutes, re-arranging them twice. Drain on paper towels and serve hot.

FREEZING DETAILS
1. Prepare the recipe to the end of step 3.
2. Freeze, interleaved with freezer film and wrapped in foil. Cover, seal, label and freeze for up to 3 months.
REHEATING DETAILS
Power Setting: Full/Maximum
Defrosting and Cooking Time: 25-29 minutes
1. Remove all wrappings and place the rissoles on a large plate. Cook on full/maximum power for 4-6 minutes, re-arranging them frequently. Leave to stand for 5 minutes.
2. Cook as in steps 4 and 5 above.

Celery with lemon and almonds;
Spinach terrine (with Provençal sauce)

CAPONATA

4 tablespoons oil
4 sticks celery, scrubbed and finely chopped
2 large onions, peeled and sliced
4 small aubergines, diced
4 tablespoons tomato purée
1 tablespoon capers
50 g (2 oz) green olives, stoned and chopped
2 tablespoons water
2 tablespoons red wine vinegar
1 teaspoon sugar
salt
freshly ground black pepper

Power Setting: Full/Maximum
Preparation and Cooking Time: 30 minutes

1. Place the oil, celery and onions in a large bowl. Cover and cook for 4 minutes, stirring once.
2. Add the aubergines, blending well. Cover and cook for 4 minutes, stirring once.
3. Stir in the remaining ingredients. Cover and cook for 6 minutes, stirring once. Leave to stand for 5 minutes.
4. Serve hot or cold with pork or chicken.

FREEZING DETAILS
1. Prepare the recipe to the end of step 3.
2. Cool quickly, spoon into a rigid container, cover, seal, label and freeze for up to 2 months.
REHEATING DETAILS
Power Setting: Defrost and Full/Maximum
Defrosting and Cooking Time: 24-31 minutes
1. Remove all wrappings and cook on defrost power for 15 minutes. If serving cold, leave to stand for 5-10 minutes.
2. To reheat, cover and cook on full/maximum power for 4-6 minutes, stirring twice.

LEEKS À LA GRECQUE

1 large onion, peeled and chopped
350 g (12 oz) leeks, washed and sliced lengthways
100 g (4 oz) button mushrooms, wiped
1 garlic clove, peeled and crushed
2 tablespoons olive oil
100 ml (3½ fl oz) dry white wine
1 x 227 g (8 oz) can peeled tomatoes
1 tablespoon tomato purée
¾ teaspoon dried mixed herbs
salt
freshly ground black pepper
To garnish:
chopped fresh basil or parsley

Power Setting: Full/Maximum
Preparation and Cooking Time: 24-26 minutes

WESTERN BAKED POTATOES

4 × 250 g (9 oz) potatoes, scrubbed
100 g (4 oz) corned beef, cubed
1 × 450 g (1 lb) can barbecue beans
salt
freshly ground black pepper
50 g (2 oz) grated cheese

Power Setting: Full/Maximum
Preparation and Cooking Time: 35 minutes

1. Prick the potatoes with a fork and arrange on a double thickness of paper towels, spaced well apart. Cook for 10 minutes, turn over and rearrange, then cook for a further 6-7 minutes. Allow to stand for 5 minutes.
2. Split each potato in half and scoop out the flesh. Mix the flesh with the corned beef, beans and salt and pepper to taste, blending well. Return the mixture to the potato skins.
3. If serving immediately, sprinkle with the cheese and cook for 3-4 minutes to reheat. Serve with barbecued meats, sausages or as a snack.

FREEZING DETAILS
1. Prepare the recipe to the end of step 2.
2. Cool quickly, place in a rigid box, cover, seal, label and freeze for up to 3 months.
REHEATING DETAILS
Power Setting: Full/Maximum
Defrosting and Cooking Time: 33-34 minutes
1. Remove all wrappings. Place the potatoes on a double thickness of paper towels, spaced well apart. Cook on defrost power for 30 minutes, rearranging them twice.
2. Sprinkle with the cheese and cook on full/maximum power for 3-4 minutes.

1. Mix the vegetables with the garlic and place in a shallow dish.
2. Mix the oil with the remaining ingredients, blending well. Spoon over the leek mixture, cover and cook for 14-16 minutes, stirring twice, until tender.
3. To serve, allow to cool, then chill. Garnish with chopped fresh basil or parsley. Serve with lamb or as a starter with crusty bread.

FREEZING DETAILS
1. Prepare the recipe to the end of step 3.
2. Cool quickly, spoon into a rigid container. Cover, seal, label and freeze for up to 3 months.
REHEATING DETAILS
Power Setting: Full/Maximum
Defrosting Time: 15 minutes
1. Remove all wrappings and place the frozen leek mixture in a bowl. Cover and cook for 5 minutes. Break up and stir well.
2. Leave to stand for 10 minutes until thoroughly thawed but still chilled. Serve garnished as above.

BROAD BEANS IN HORSERADISH CREAM

450 g (1 lb) shelled broad beans
4 tablespoons water
salt
25 g (1 oz) butter
2 tablespoons plain flour
300 ml (½ pint) milk
4 tablespoons double cream
4 teaspoons horseradish sauce
pinch of caster sugar
freshly ground black pepper
To garnish:
chopped fresh parsley

Power Setting: Full/Maximum
Preparation and Cooking Time: 20 minutes

1. Place the broad beans in a bowl with the water and a little salt. Cover and cook for 6-8 minutes, shaking the dish once. Leave to stand while preparing the sauce.

2. Place the butter in a bowl and cook for ½ minute to melt. Stir in the flour, blending well. Gradually add the milk and cook for 4-4½ minutes, stirring every 1 minute until smooth and thickened.

3. Add the remaining ingredients, blending thoroughly.

4. Fold in the drained cooked beans, tossing well to coat.

5. To serve immediately, cook for 1-2 minutes to reheat. Sprinkle with chopped parsley and serve.

FREEZING DETAILS

1. Prepare the recipe to the end of step 4.

2. Cool quickly, spoon into a rigid container. Cover, seal, label and freeze for up to 3 months.

REHEATING DETAILS

Power Setting: Full/Maximum
Defrosting and Cooking Time: 15 minutes

1. Remove all wrappings. Place the frozen bean mixture in a bowl, cover and cook on full/maximum power for 7 minutes, breaking up the beans and stirring twice. Leave to stand for 5 minutes.

2. Cook on full/maximum power for 3 minutes, stirring once. Serve sprinkled with chopped parsley.

Broad beans in horseradish cream;
Caponata; Western baked potatoes

VEGETABLES RAJAH

4 medium potatoes, peeled and sliced
4 large carrots, peeled and sliced
6 small turnips, peeled and sliced
1 × 425 g (15 oz) can Madras hot curry cook-in sauce
1 × 227 g (8 oz) can plum tomatoes
3 onions, peeled and sliced
1 small green pepper, cored, seeded and sliced
1 large garlic clove, peeled and finely chopped
1 tablespoon chopped stem ginger
100 g (4 oz) frozen petits pois
100 ml (3½ fl oz) plain unsweetened yogurt
3 tablespoons chopped fresh mint
To garnish:
sprig of fresh mint

Power Setting: Full/Maximum and Medium
Preparation and Cooking Time: 55 minutes

1. Place the potatoes, carrots, turnips, curry sauce and tomatoes with their juice in a large casserole, blending well. Cover and cook on full/maximum power for 15 minutes, stirring once.
2. Add the onions, pepper, garlic, ginger and peas. Cover and cook on full/maximum power for a further 10 minutes, stirring the vegetables once.
3. Cover and cook on medium power for a further 20 minutes until the vegetables are fork tender.
4. To serve immediately, stir in the yogurt and mint and garnish with mint. Serve hot with boiled rice, poppadums, chutneys as part of an Indian meal, or increase the quantities and serve with a simple mixed green salad.

FREEZING DETAILS
1. Prepare the recipe to the end of step 3.
2. Cool quickly and spoon into a rigid container, cover, seal, label and freeze for up to 2 months.
REHEATING DETAILS
Power Setting: Defrost and Full/Maximum
Defrosting and Cooking Time: 47 minutes
1. Remove all wrappings and place the frozen curry in a serving dish. Cover and cook on defrost power for 25 minutes, stirring once. Leave to stand for 10 minutes.
2. Cook on full/maximum power for 12 minutes, stirring once. Stir in the yogurt and mint and garnish with mint. Serve hot as above.

ARTICHOKE MOUSSELINE

6 globe artichokes
250 ml (8 fl oz) half milk and half water mixed
salt
1½ tablespoons lemon juice
3 tablespoons double cream
freshly ground black pepper
40 g (1½ oz) butter to serve
To garnish:
sprigs of fresh parsley or chervil

Power Setting: Full/Maximum
Preparation and Cooking Time: 30 minutes

1. Remove the leaves from the artichokes, discarding the chokes but keeping the hearts. Trim away any woody or dry parts from the leaves.
2. Rinse, then place in a bowl with the water and milk, a pinch of salt and the lemon juice. Cover and cook for 16-18 minutes, stirring twice, until tender. Drain thoroughly, reserving the cooking juices.
3. Purée the artichokes (together with the trimmed leaves) in a blender until smooth. Add the cream and salt and pepper to taste, blending well. If necessary, add 2-3 tablespoons of the cooking juices to produce a smooth creamy texture.
4. Spoon into a serving dish and fork attractively, or spoon into a piping bag fitted with a large star nozzle and pipe attractively into a serving dish.
5. To serve immediately, cover and cook for 2-4 minutes to reheat. Dot with the butter and garnish with the parsley or chervil sprigs. Serve with veal, pork or gammon.

FREEZING DETAILS
1. Prepare the recipe to the end of step 3.
2. Cool quickly, cover, seal, label and freeze for up to 2 months.
REHEATING DETAILS
Power Setting: Defrost and Full/Maximum
Defrosting and Cooking Time: 21-22 minutes
1. Remove all wrappings. Cover and cook on defrost power for 12 minutes. Leave to stand for 5 minutes.
2. Cook on full/maximum power for 4-5 minutes.
3. To serve, dot with the butter and garnish with the chervil or parsley sprigs.

Vegetables rajah;
Artichoke mousseline

CREAMED MUSHROOMS

450 g (1 lb) field, oyster or cap mushrooms, wiped
25 g (1 oz) butter
4 tablespoons plain flour
200 ml (7 fl oz) milk
1 tablespoon chopped fresh parsley
25 g (1 oz) grated cheese
salt
freshly ground black pepper
pinch of ground nutmeg
4 large slices buttered toast to serve
To garnish:
sprigs of fresh parsley

Power Setting: Full/Maximum
Preparation and Cooking Time: 15 minutes

1. Cut the mushrooms into bite-sized pieces if large, leave them whole if small.
2. Place the butter in a bowl and cook for ½ minute to melt. Add the mushroom pieces, cover and cook for 4 minutes until tender, stirring once.

3. Stir the flour into the juices, blending well. Cook for ½ minute. Gradually add the milk and cook for 5-6 minutes, stirring every 1 minute until smooth and thickened.
4. Stir in the parsley and the cheese until melted. Add salt, pepper and nutmeg to taste.
5. To serve immediately, spoon on to slices of hot buttered toast and garnish with fresh parsley. Serve as an accompaniment to a mixed grill, or steak.

FREEZING DETAILS
1. Prepare the recipe to the end of step 4.
2. Cool quickly, spoon into a rigid container, cover, seal, label and freeze for up to 1 month.

REHEATING DETAILS
Power Setting: Full/Maximum
Defrosting and Cooking Time: 13-14 minutes
1. Remove all wrappings. Place the frozen mushroom mixture in a bowl and cook, uncovered, for 5 minutes, stirring once. Leave to stand for 5 minutes.
2. Cook for 3-4 minutes, stirring once until hot and bubbly.
3. Spoon on to slices of hot buttered toast and garnish with fresh parsley.

SPECIAL DINNERS

GAMMON IN CHERRY SAUCE

Serves 6-8
1 × 1.75 kg (4 lb) gammon joint
1 × 425 g (15 oz) can black cherries
about 150 ml (¼ pint) red wine
2 teaspoons arrowroot powder
1 teaspoon lemon juice

Power Setting: Full/Maximum and Medium
Preparation and Cooking Time: about 1¼ hours

1. Preheat a large browning dish on full/maximum power for 8 minutes (or according to the manufacturer's instructions).
2. Meanwhile, using a sharp knife, peel the rind from the gammon and score the fat in a diamond pattern.
3. Add the gammon joint to the dish and turn quickly on the fat side to brown evenly. Remove and place on a roasting rack. Cook on medium power for 38-42 minutes, turning the rack occasionally. Cover with aluminium foil and leave to stand.
4. Meanwhile, drain the juice from the cherries into a heatproof measuring jug and make up to 300 ml (½ pint) with red wine.
5. Cut the cherries in half and remove and discard the stones.
6. Mix the arrowroot powder with a little of the cherry juice mixture and lemon juice, then stir into the jug. Cook on full/maximum power for 3-4 minutes, stirring every 1 minute. Add the cherries, blending well. (Add a little sugar if wished.)
7. Carve the gammon and spoon over the sauce.

FREEZING DETAILS
1. Prepare the recipe to the end of step 6.
2. Cool quickly, wrap the gammon in aluminium foil and pack the sauce separately. Cover, seal, label and freeze for up to 2 months.

REHEATING DETAILS
Power Setting: Defrost and Full/Maximum
Defrosting and Cooking Time: 56-71 minutes
1. Remove all wrappings. Place the gammon on a roasting rack and cook on defrost power for 25 minutes. Leave to stand for 20-30 minutes.
2. Place the frozen sauce in a jug and cook on full/maximum power for 5-6 minutes, stirring twice.
3. Reheat the cooked gammon by cooking on full/maximum power for 6-10 minutes.
4. Serve as in step 7 above.

BEEF IN GINGER WINE

1 kg (2 lb) lean braising steak
50 g (2 oz) seasoned flour
2 tablespoons oil
6 carrots, peeled and cut into thick strips
5 celery sticks, sliced into thick strips
1 bunch watercress, washed, sorted and coarsely chopped
salt
freshly ground black pepper
300 ml (½ pint) ginger wine
1-2 teaspoons cornflour (optional)
To garnish:
sprigs of watercress

Power Setting: Full/Maximum and Medium
Preparation and Cooking Time: about 1½ hours

1. Preheat a large browning dish on full/maximum power for 8 minutes (or according to the manufacturer's instructions).
2. Meanwhile cut the meat into large cubes and toss in the flour.
3. Brush the dish with oil and cook on full/maximum power for 1 minute. Add the beef, turning quickly on all sides to brown evenly. Cook on full/maximum power for 5 minutes, turning once.
4. Place the vegetables in a large casserole. Sprinkle with salt and pepper. Add the meat and pour over the ginger wine. Cover and cook on full/maximum power for 10 minutes.
5. Reduce the power setting to medium and cook for a further 40-50 minutes, stirring once, until fork-tender.
6. Thicken with the cornflour dissolved in a little water (if used). Leave to stand for 5 minutes. Serve garnished with watercress.

FREEZING DETAILS
1. Prepare the recipe to the end of step 5.
2. Cool quickly, seal, label and freeze for up to 1 month.
REHEATING DETAILS
Power Setting: Defrost and Full/Maximum
Defrosting and Cooking Time: 35-37 minutes
1. Cook, covered, on defrost power for 20 minutes, stirring once. Leave to stand for 5 minutes.
2. Cook on full/maximum power for 10-12 minutes, stirring twice. Thicken with the cornflour dissolved in a little water (if used). Serve garnished with watercress.

Gammon in cherry sauce; Beef in ginger wine

SMOKED HADDOCK MOUSSE

Serves 4-6

225 g (8 oz) smoked haddock fillet
1 tablespoon water
15 g (½ oz) powdered gelatine
150 ml (¼ pint) chicken stock
1½ tablespoons lemon juice
75 g (3 oz) Gouda cheese, grated
freshly ground black pepper
75 g (3 oz) butter
1 tablespoon chopped fresh parsley

To garnish:

lemon wedges
cucumber slices
tomato slices
mustard and cress

Power Setting: Full/Maximum
Preparation and Cooking Time: 20 minutes, plus chilling

1. Place the haddock in a dish with the water. Cover and cook for 3-3½ minutes. Allow to cool slightly, skin and flake the haddock into a blender goblet.
2. Meanwhile, mix the gelatine with the stock and leave to soften for 2 minutes. Cook for 1 minute until the gelatine is clear and dissolved. Add to the blender goblet.
3. Add the lemon juice, cheese and pepper to taste. Purée until smooth.
4. Place the butter in a bowl and cook for 1¼ minutes to melt. Stir into the haddock mixture with the parsley, blending well. Pour into a small greased ring mould and chill until set.
5. To serve, dip the mould briefly into hot water and turn the mousse on to a serving plate. Garnish with lemon wedges, cucumber and tomato slices and small bunches of mustard and cress in the centre. Serve as a starter.

FREEZING DETAILS

1. Prepare the recipe to the end of step 4.
2. Cover the mould with aluminium foil, seal, label and freeze for up to 2 months.

DEFROSTING DETAILS

Power Setting: Defrost
Defrosting Time: 30 minutes

1. Remove all wrappings. Dip the mould briefly into hot water and turn the mousse on to a serving plate. Cook on defrost power for 10 minutes. Leave to stand for 20 minutes.
2. Garnish with lemon wedges, cucumber and tomato slices and small bunches of mustard and cress in the centre.

HAM AND MUSHROOM COCOTTES

Cocottes:

25 g (1 oz) butter
1 onion, peeled and chopped
25 g (1 oz) plain flour
300 ml (½ pint) ham stock
2 tablespoons single cream
salt
freshly ground black pepper
100 g (4 oz) button mushrooms, wiped and very finely sliced
225 g (8 oz) cooked ham, cubed

Croûtons:

50 g (2 oz) butter
75 g (3 oz) bread, crusts removed, cut into cubes

To garnish:

sprigs of fresh parsley

Power Setting: Full/Maximum
Preparation and Cooking Time: 20 minutes

1. Place the butter in a bowl and cook for 1 minute to melt. Add the onion, cover and cook for 3 minutes.
2. Stir in the flour, mixing well. Gradually add the stock and cook for 3½-4 minutes, stirring every 1 minute, until smooth and thickened.
3. Stir in the cream and salt and pepper to taste, blending well. Fold in the mushrooms and ham.
4. Spoon into 4 cocotte dishes, cover and cook for 2 minutes.
5. To serve immediately, place the butter for the croûtons in a large bowl. Cook for ¾-1 minute to melt. Add the bread cubes and toss to coat. Cook for 1½ minutes, stir and cook for a further 1½ minutes. Sprinkle the croûtons over the cocottes and serve as a starter garnished with parsley.

FREEZING DETAILS

1. Prepare the recipe to the end of step 4.
2. Cool quickly, cover, seal, label and freeze for up to 3 months.

REHEATING DETAILS

Power Setting: Defrost and Full/Maximum
Defrosting and Cooking Time: 22-23 minutes

1. Remove all wrappings. Cook on defrost power for 10 minutes. Leave to stand for 5 minutes.
2. Cook on full/maximum power for 3-4 minutes to reheat.
3. Cook the croûtons as in step 5 above. Sprinkle over the cocottes and serve garnished with parsley.

Smoked haddock mousse;
Ham and mushroom cocottes

TAGLIATELLE WITH WALNUT SAUCE

350 g (12 oz) green tagliatelle
900 ml (1 ½ pints) boiling water
salt
1 teaspoon oil
50 g (2 oz) butter
4 tablespoons soured cream
Walnut sauce:
6 tablespoons olive oil
2 garlic cloves, peeled and crushed
100 g (4 oz) walnuts, chopped
75 g (3 oz) grated Parmesan cheese

Power Setting: Full/Maximum
Preparation and Cooking Time: 20 minutes

1. Place the pasta in a deep bowl with the boiling water, a little salt and the oil. Cover with cling film, snipping 2 holes in the top to allow any steam to escape. Cook for 6 minutes. Allow to stand for 3 minutes.

2. To serve immediately, make the walnut sauce. Place the oil in a bowl and cook for 1-2 minutes until hot. Add the garlic and walnuts and cook for 2-4 minutes or until the mixture browns slightly. Stir in the Parmesan cheese. Keep hot while finishing the tagliatelle.

3. Place the butter in a bowl and cook for 1 minute to melt. Drain the cooked tagliatelle and toss in the melted butter.

4. Spoon the tagliatelle into a hot serving dish and top with the soured cream. Serve as a starter with the hot walnut sauce.

FREEZING DETAILS

1. Prepare the recipe to the end of step 1.

2. Drain the tagliatelle and cool quickly. Pack in a rigid container, cover, seal, label and freeze for up to 1 month.

REHEATING DETAILS

Power Setting: Defrost and Full/Maximum
Defrosting and Cooking Time: 21-26 minutes

1. Remove all wrappings. Place the pasta in a serving dish. Cook on defrost power for 8 minutes. Leave to stand for 3 minutes.

2. Cook on full/maximum power for 4-6 minutes. Leave to stand for 2 minutes. Continue from step 2 above.

TURKEY WITH CRANBERRY STUFFING

---

1 × 4.5 kg (10 lb) fresh oven-ready turkey

Stuffing:

25 g (1 oz) butter
1 large onion, peeled and chopped
3 celery sticks, scrubbed and chopped
175 g (6 oz) dry white breadcrumbs
grated rind of ½ lemon
1½ tablespoons lemon juice
grated rind of 1 orange
4 tablespoons orange juice
1 × 175 g (6 oz) jar cranberry sauce with wine
2 teaspoons dried mixed herbs
salt
freshly ground black pepper
1 egg, beaten

Glaze:

50 g (2 oz) butter
3 tablespoons cranberry sauce with wine

To garnish

bacon rolls
sprigs of watercress (see below)

Power Setting: Full/Maximum
Preparation and Cooking Time: about 1¾ hours

1. Prepare the stuffing by placing the butter in a bowl. Cook for ½ minute to melt. Add the onion and celery. Cover and cook for 4½-5 minutes or until softened. Add the breadcrumbs, lemon rind, lemon juice, orange rind, orange juice, cranberry sauce with wine, herbs and salt and pepper to taste, blending well. Bind together with the beaten egg.

2. Stuff the turkey with the mixture, securing with wooden cocktail sticks.

3. To serve immediately, mix the butter for the glaze with the cranberry sauce with wine and salt and pepper to taste. Using a small knife, carefully loosen the breast skin from the flesh of the turkey by the legs. Using a teaspoon, insert the glaze mixture into the cavities under the skin on each breast (see right).

4. Shield the turkey wings with small pieces of aluminium foil (see note on shielding, page 6). Place the turkey on a roasting rack or

large upturned saucer in a roasting dish. Place in a roasting bag if preferred, securing the end with string or an elastic band.

5. Cook for 1¼-1½ hours, turning the dish every 15 minutes and basting occasionally with the juices. Cover with aluminium foil and leave to stand for 15 minutes before carving.

6. Roll up pieces of bacon and serve with cocktail sticks. Cook for 2-3 minutes. Serve the turkey garnished with the bacon rolls and watercress.

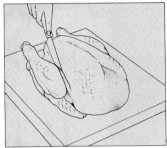

Carefully slit the breast skin by the legs and loosen the skin with your hands.

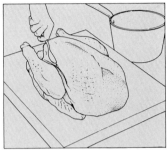

Using a teaspoon, insert the glaze into the pockets on each breast.

FREEZING DETAILS
1. Prepare the recipe to the end of step 2.
2. Freeze the uncooked stuffed turkey without its glaze, wrapped in aluminium foil and labelled, for up to 3 months.
COOKING DETAILS
Power Setting: Defrost and Full/Maximum
Defrosting and Cooking Time: 2¾-3¼ hours
1. Remove all wrappings and cook on defrost power for 1½-1¾ hours, turning over twice. Shield any warm spots with small strips of aluminium foil if necessary (see note on shielding, page 6).
2. Glaze and cook from step 3 above.
3. Serve garnished with bacon rolls and watercress sprigs.

DANISH STROGANOFF

3 × 175 g (6 oz) unsmoked gammon steaks
50 g (2 oz) butter
1 onion, peeled and sliced
225 g (8 oz) button mushrooms, sliced
25 g (1 oz) plain flour
1 tablespoon tomato purée
150 ml (¼ pint) ham or light chicken stock or dry white wine
salt
freshly ground black pepper
150 ml (¼ pint) soured cream
To garnish:
chopped fresh parsley

Power Setting: Full/Maximum
Preparation and Cooking Time: 15-20 minutes

1. Remove the rinds from the gammon and cut into thin strips.
2. Place the butter in a bowl and cook for ½-1 minute to melt. Add the gammon and cook for 4 minutes.
3. Add the onion and mushrooms. Cover and cook for 4 minutes, stirring once. Remove the gammon and reserve.
4. Stir in the flour and tomato purée, blending well. Gradually add the stock or wine and reserved gammon. Cook for 1½ minutes stirring once. Add salt and pepper to taste.
5. To serve immediately, stir in the soured cream, sprinkle with chopped parsley and serve hot, with noodles or rice.

FREEZING DETAILS
1. Prepare the recipe to the end of step 4.
2. Cool quickly, pack into a rigid container, cover, seal, label and freeze for up to 2 months.
REHEATING DETAILS
Power Setting: Defrost and Full/Maximum
Defrosting and Cooking Time: 25-30 minutes
1. Remove all wrappings. Cook on defrost power for 8-10 minutes. Leave to stand for 10 minutes.
2. Cover and cook on full/maximum power for 7-10 minutes to reheat, stirring twice.
3. Stir in the soured cream and sprinkle with chopped parsley.

Turkey with cranberry stuffing;
Danish stroganoff

*Sizzling beef steaks with tomato sauce;
Duck in mustard sauce*

SIZZLING BEEF STEAKS WITH TOMATO SAUCE

4 thin slices blade steak
25 g (1 oz) seasoned flour
1 tablespoon oil
Tomato sauce:
25 g (1 oz) butter
1 onion, peeled and sliced
1 small garlic clove, peeled and crushed
6 tomatoes, peeled, seeded and chopped
¼ teaspoon dried thyme or ½ teaspoon chopped fresh thyme
150 ml (¼ pint) beef stock
salt
freshly ground black pepper
To garnish:
sprigs of fresh thyme

Power Setting: Full/Maximum
Preparation and Cooking Time: 30 minutes

1. Place the blade steaks between sheets of cling film and beat with a rolling pin until paper-thin. Coat in the seasoned flour.
2. Meanwhile, prepare the sauce by placing the butter in a bowl. Cook for ½ minute to melt. Add the onion and garlic, cover and cook for 3 minutes.
3. Add the tomatoes, thyme, stock and salt and pepper to taste, blending well. Cover and cook for 3 minutes, stirring once.
4. Preheat a large browning dish for 8 minutes (or according to the manufacturer's instructions). Brush with the oil and cook for a further 1 minute. Add the steaks and turn quickly on all sides to brown evenly.
5. To serve immediately, spoon over the sauce and cook for 3-4 minutes. Garnish with thyme and serve with boiled rice.

FREEZING DETAILS
1. Prepare the recipe to the end of step 4.
2. Place the steaks in a rigid container and spoon over the sauce. Cool quickly, cover, seal, label and freeze for up to 3 months.
REHEATING DETAILS
Power Setting: Defrost and Full/Maximum
Defrosting and Cooking Time: 26-28 minutes
1. Remove all wrappings. Cook on defrost power for 9-11 minutes. Leave to stand for 10 minutes.
2. Cook on full/maximum power for 7 minutes.
3. Garnish with thyme and serve with boiled rice.

DUCK IN MUSTARD SAUCE

1 × 2 kg (4½ lb) oven-ready duckling, trussed
salt
freshly ground black pepper
Mustard sauce:
25 g (1 oz) butter
1 duck's liver
1 onion, peeled and chopped
100 ml (4 fl oz) red wine
1½ tablespoons lemon juice
grated rind of 1 small lemon
1-2 teaspoons Dijon mustard
To garnish:
sprigs of watercress

Power Setting: Medium and Full/Maximum
Preparation and Cooking Time: about 1-1¼ hours

1. Prick the skin of the duck and sprinkle with salt and pepper to taste. Shield the tips of the wings, tail end and legs of the duck with small pieces of aluminium foil (see note on shielding, page 6). Place, breast side down, on a roasting rack or upturned saucer in a dish. Cook on medium power for 25 minutes.
2. Drain away any cooking juices and reserve 4 tablespoons in a bowl. Turn the duck over and cook on medium power, for a further 15-24 minutes, until cooked. Remove from the oven and leave to stand, wrapped in aluminium foil, for 10 minutes.
3. Meanwhile, make the sauce. Place the butter in a bowl and cook on full/maximum power for ½ minute to melt. Add the duck's liver, cover and cook for ½-1 minute. Remove with slotted spoon and mash to a smooth paste.
4. Add the onion to the reserved juices. Cover and cook on full/maximum power for 3 minutes. Stir in the wine, lemon juice, lemon rind and mustard to taste. Cook on full power for 2-3 minutes, until boiling. Beat in the duck's liver to blend well.
5. Carve the duck into portions and serve coated with the sauce.
6. Garnish with watercress sprigs.

FREEZING DETAILS

1. Prepare the recipe to the end of step 5.
2. Cool quickly, place the duck coated with sauce, in a rigid container, cover, seal, label and freeze for up to 1 month.
REHEATING DETAILS
Power Setting: Defrost and Full/Maximum
Defrosting and Cooking Time: 45-50 minutes
1. Remove all wrappings. Place the duck and sauce in a serving dish and cook on defrost power for 25 minutes. Leave to stand for 10 minutes.
2. Cook on full/maximum power for 10-15 minutes, turning and re-arranging occasionally. Garnish with watercress sprigs.

PORK WITH LEMON AND TARRAGON SAUCE

1 tablespoon oil
1 × 1.75 kg (4 lb) loin of pork, boned and rolled
Tarragon sauce:
1 tablespoon plain flour
grated rind of 1 large lemon
4 tablespoons lemon juice
2 teaspoons chopped fresh tarragon or 1 teaspoon dried
  tarragon
150 ml (¼ pint) white meat stock
salt
freshly ground black pepper
1 tablespoon double cream

Power Setting: Full/Maximum and Medium
Preparation and Cooking Time: about 1¼ hours

1. Preheat a large browning dish on full/maximum power for 8 minutes (or according to the manufacturer's instructions). Brush with the oil and cook on full/maximum power for a further 1 minute.
2. Add the pork and turn quickly on all sides to brown evenly. Cook on medium power for 45-50 minutes, turning the dish occasionally.
3. Remove from the browning dish, wrap in aluminium foil and leave to stand while making the sauce.
4. Pour off all but 2 tablespoons of the juices from the dish. Stir in the flour, lemon rind, lemon juice and tarragon, blending well. Cook on full power for 1 minute.
5. Gradually add the stock and salt and pepper to taste, blending well. Cook on full/maximum power for 2-3 minutes, stirring once.
6. If serving immediately, stir the cream into the sauce. Serve the cooked loin of pork sliced, with the sauce separately.

FREEZING DETAILS

1. Prepare the recipe to the end of step 5.
2. Cool the pork and wrap in aluminium foil. Place the sauce (without the cream) in a rigid container. Cover, seal, label and freeze for up to 2 months.
REHEATING DETAILS
Power Setting: Defrost and Full/Maximum
Defrosting and Cooking Time: 46-50 minutes
1. Remove all wrappings. Cover and cook the pork in a serving dish on defrost power for 25 minutes. Leave to stand for 10 minutes.
2. Place the frozen sauce in a serving dish and cook on full/maximum power for 3-5 minutes, stirring twice. Stir in the cream, blending well.
3. Cook the pork on full/maximum power for 8-10 minutes.
4. Carve the pork into slices and serve with the sauce separately.

LEMON AND HERB MARINATED LAMB CHOPS

4 large 'butterfly' or double-loin lamb chops
Marinade:
4 tablespoons olive oil
grated rind of 1 lemon
3 tablespoons lemon juice
1 tablespoon chopped fresh parsley
1 tablespoon dried herbes de Provence
1 garlic clove, peeled and crushed
4 bay leaves
salt
freshly ground black pepper
Vegetables:
1 head celery, trimmed and sliced
1 small onion, peeled and chopped
25 g (1 oz) butter
5 teaspoons water
½ teaspoon salt
350 g (12 oz) frozen peas
To garnish:
celery leaves

**Power Setting: Full/Maximum and Medium
Preparation and Cooking Time: 35 minutes, plus
marinating**

1. Place the chops in a shallow dish. Mix the marinade ingredients together and pour over the chops. Cover and leave to marinate for 4-5 hours.
2. Place the celery, onion, butter, water and salt in a large dish. Cover and cook on full/maximum power for 6 minutes. Add the peas, cover and cook, on full/maximum power for 7-8 minutes, stirring once. Cover and leave to stand while cooking the chops.
3. Preheat a large browning dish on full/maximum power for 8 minutes (or according to the manufacturer's instructions). Drain the chops from the marinade with a slotted spoon and add to the browning dish, turning quickly on all sides to brown evenly. Cook on full/maximum power for 1½ minutes. Turn over and cook on medium power for 1½-2 minutes.
4. To serve immediately, place the cooked vegetables on a preheated serving dish and top with the cooked lamb chops. Garnish with celery leaves.

FREEZING DETAILS
1. Prepare the recipe to the end of step 3.
2. Place the vegetables in a rigid container and top with the chops.
3. Cool quickly, cover, seal, label and freeze for up to 1 month.
REHEATING DETAILS
Power Setting: Defrost and Full/Maximum
Defrosting and Cooking Time: 28-32 minutes
1. Remove all wrappings. Cook on defrost power for 10-12 minutes. Leave to stand for 10 minutes.
2. Cook on full/maximum power for 8-10 minutes, stirring and re-arranging once. Garnish with celery leaves.

MONKFISH IN TOMATO AND COGNAC SAUCE

900 g (2 lb) monkfish tails
25 g (1 oz) butter
1 carrot, peeled and very finely chopped
1 small onion, peeled and very finely chopped
2 shallots, peeled and very finely chopped
1 garlic clove, peeled and crushed
150 ml (¼ pint) dry white wine
2 tablespoons cognac
225 g (8 oz) tomatoes, peeled, seeded and chopped
1 teaspoon tomato purée
120-150 ml (4-5 fl oz) fish stock or dry white wine
2 teaspoons cornflour
salt
freshly ground black pepper
lemon juice
To garnish:
fresh dill

**Power Setting: Full/Maximum
Preparation and Cooking Time: 35 minutes**

1. Prepare the monkfish tails by removing the flesh, in two pieces, from the central bone and slice into bite-sized pieces.
2. Place the butter in a large bowl and cook for ½ minute to melt. Add the monkfish pieces, cover and cook for 8 minutes, stirring the pieces twice.
3. Remove the monkfish with a slotted spoon and reserve.
4. Add the carrot, onion, shallots and garlic to the juices. Cover and cook for 5 minutes, stirring once.
5. Add the wine, cognac, tomatoes and tomato purée, blending well. Cover and cook for 4 minutes.
6. Mix the fish stock or wine, according to required consistency, with the cornflour and stir into the tomato mixture with salt, pepper and lemon juice to taste. Cover and cook for 2-3 minutes, stirring twice. Add the monkfish pieces.
7. To serve immediately, cook for 2 minutes to reheat. Garnish with fresh dill and serve with boiled rice.

FREEZING DETAILS
1. Prepare the recipe to the end of step 6.
2. Cool quickly, spoon into a rigid container, cover, seal, label and freeze for up to 1 month.
REHEATING DETAILS
Power Setting: Defrost and Full/Maximum
Defrosting and Cooking Time: 26-28 minutes
1. Remove all wrappings. Cook on defrost power for 15 minutes. Leave to stand for 5 minutes.
2. Cook on full/maximum power for 6-8 minutes. Garnish with fresh dill and serve with boiled rice.

CLOKWISE FROM BOTTOM LEFT: Lemon and herb marinated lamb chops; Beef and mango korma (with banana and yogurt accompaniment); Monkfish in tomato and cognac sauce

BEEF AND MANGO KORMA

Serves 4-6

1.25 kg (2½ lb) chuck steak, cubed
1 × 425 g (15 oz) can medium curry cook-in sauce
120 ml (4 fl oz) beef stock
100 g (4 oz) desiccated coconut
150 ml (¼ pint) single cream
100 g (4 oz) seedless raisins
1 × 425 g (15 oz) can mango slices, drained or 2 large
  mangoes, peeled, stoned and sliced

Power Setting: Full/Maximum and Medium
Preparation and Cooking Time: about 1 hour

1. Place the beef in a large casserole with the curry sauce, stock, coconut, cream and raisins, blending very well. Cover and cook on full/maximum power for 15 minutes, stirring once.

2. Reduce the power setting to medium, cover and cook for a further 20 minutes, stirring twice.

3. Add the mango slices, blending well. Cover and cook on medium power for a further 15-20 minutes until the meat is tender. Leave to stand for 5 minutes.

4. Serve with boiled rice, poppadums, sliced bananas in yogurt (dipped in lemon juice first) and spicy mango chutney.

FREEZING DETAILS

1. Prepare the recipe to the end of step 3.

2. Cool quickly, cover, seal, label and freeze for up to 2 months.

REHEATING DETAILS

Power Setting: Defrost and Full/Maximum
Defrosting and Cooking Time: 38-40 minutes

1. Remove all wrappings. Cover and cook on defrost power for 25 minutes. Leave to stand for 5 minutes.

2. Cook on full/maximum power for 8-10 minutes, stirring once.

3. Serve as in step 4, above.

TIPSY TURKEY

4 turkey fillets or escalopes
salt
freshly ground black pepper
1 tablespoon oil
Sauce:
25 g (1 oz) butter
1 onion, peeled and sliced
1 red pepper, cored, seeded and sliced
1 tablespoon plain flour
200 ml (7 fl oz) lager or pale ale
150 ml (¼ pint) chicken stock
½ teaspoon dried thyme
1 teaspoon sugar
4 tablespoons single cream
To garnish:
red pepper rings
sprigs of fresh parsley

Power Setting: Full/Maximum
Preparation and Cooking Time: 30-35 minutes

1. Prepare the sauce by placing the butter in a bowl. Cook for ½ minute to melt. Add the onion and red pepper, cover and cook for 4 minutes.
2. Stir the flour into the butter, blending well, then gradually add the lager or pale ale and stock. Stir in the thyme and sugar with salt and pepper to taste. Cover and cook for 4-6 minutes, stirring every 1 minute until boiling and thickened.
3. Meanwhile, split the turkey fillets or escalopes in half, through the centre, to give 8 thick slices. Sprinkle generously with salt and pepper.
4. Preheat a large browning dish for 8 minutes (or according to the manufacturer's instructions). Brush with the oil and cook for a further 1 minute. Add the turkey slices and turn quickly on all sides to brown evenly.
5. To serve immediately, spoon over the sauce and cook for 4-6 minutes. Stir in the cream, blending well. Garnish with pepper rings and parsley.

FREEZING DETAILS
1. Prepare the recipe to the end of step 4.
2. Place the turkey slices in a rigid container and spoon over the sauce. Cool quickly, cover, seal, label and freeze for up to 3 months.
REHEATING DETAILS
Power Setting: Defrost and Full/Maximum
Defrosting and Cooking Time: 26-30 minutes
1. Remove all wrappings, cook on defrost power for 9-11 minutes. Leave to stand for 10 minutes.
2. Cook on full/maximum power for 7-9 minutes. Stir in the cream, blending well. Garnish with pepper rings and parsley.

FRENCH-STYLE LAMB

550 g (1 ¼ lb) lamb fillet, cubed
40 g (1 ½ oz) butter
1 tablespoon plain flour
Marinade:
250 ml (8 fl oz) red wine
2 carrots, peeled and sliced
2 onions, peeled and roughly cut into chunks
1 teaspoon dried thyme
1 bay leaf
small piece of orange rind
salt
freshly ground black pepper
40 g (1 ½ oz) butter
1 tablespoon plain flour

Power Setting: Full/Maximum and Defrost
Preparation and Cooking Time: 35 minutes, plus marinating

1. Place the lamb and marinade ingredients in a bowl. Cover and leave to marinate for 3 hours.
2. Drain the wine from the meat mixture and set aside.
3. Place the butter in a casserole and cook on full power for ½ minute to melt. Blend in the flour and cook on full/maximum power for 1 minute. Gradually add the reserved wine, blending well. Stir in the meat mixture. Cover tightly and cook on full/maximum power for 15 minutes, stirring twice.
4. Reduce the power setting to defrost and cook for a further 10 minutes. Remove and discard the bay leaf and orange rind.
5. Serve hot with baked potatoes (page 48, omitting the filling) and vegetables in season.

FREEZING DETAILS
1. Prepare the recipe to the end of step 4.
2. Cool quickly, cover, seal, label and freeze for up to 2 months.
REHEATING DETAILS
Power Setting: Defrost and Full/Maximum
Defrosting and Cooking Time: 33-35 minutes
1. Remove all wrappings. Cook on defrost power for 20 minutes. Leave to stand for 5 minutes.
2. Cook on full/maximum power for 8-10 minutes, stirring once.
3. Serve hot with baked potatoes (page 48, omitting the filling) and vegetables in season.

Tipsy turkey; Sherried kidneys

SHERRIED KIDNEYS

25 g (1 oz) butter
1 small onion, peeled and finely chopped
550 g (1 ¼ lb) lambs' kidneys, skinned, halved and cored
120 ml (4 fl oz) beef stock
1 teaspoon French mustard
2 tablespoons dry sherry
2 tablespoons smooth liver pâté
salt
freshly ground black pepper
To garnish:
chopped fresh parsley

Power Setting: Full/Maximum
Preparation and Cooking Time: 25 minutes

1. Place the butter in a medium casserole and cook for ½ minute to melt. Add the onion, cover and cook for 2 minutes.

2. Stir in the kidneys, cover and cook for 6-8 minutes, stirring them once.

3. Add the stock, mustard, sherry, pâté and salt and pepper to taste, blending well. Cover and cook for 2-3 minutes until hot, bubbly and the kidneys are cooked through. Allow to stand for 3-5 minutes.

4. Serve with boiled rice sprinkled with chopped parsley.

FREEZING DETAILS
1. Prepare the recipe to the end of step 3.
2. Cool quickly, cover, seal, label and freeze for up to 1 month.
REHEATING DETAILS
Power Setting: Defrost and Full/Maximum
Defrosting and Cooking Time: 24-26 minutes
1. Remove all wrappings. Cook on defrost power for 10 minutes. Leave to stand for 10 minutes.
2. Cook on full/maximum power for 4-6 minutes, stirring once.
3. Serve with boiled rice sprinkled with chopped parsley.

CHOCOLATE BRANDY MOUSSE

2-3 tablespoons sugar
2 tablespoons custard powder
600 ml (1 pint) milk
vanilla essence
100 g (4 oz) plain chocolate, broken into squares
7 g (¼ oz) powdered gelatine
2 tablespoons water
2 tablespoons brandy
150 ml (¼ pint) double or whipping cream
To decorate:
whipped cream
chocolate curls

Power Setting: Full/Maximum
Preparation and Cooking Time: about 20 minutes, plus cooling and chilling

1. In a large jug or bowl, mix sugar to taste with the custard powder and a little of the milk. Gradually add the remaining milk and cook for 5-6 minutes, stirring every 1 minute, until smooth and thick. Add a few drops of vanilla essence, blending well. Allow the mixture to cool.

2. Place the chocolate in a bowl and cook for 2-3 minutes to melt.

3. Meanwhile, mix the gelatine with the water in a small jug and leave until the liquid is absorbed.

4. Cook for ½ minute or until dissolved. Stir the melted chocolate, dissolved gelatine and brandy into the custard, blending well.

5. Whip the cream until it stands in soft peaks. Fold into the custard mixture with a metal spoon. Spoon into a serving dish or individual glasses and chill to set.

6. To serve immediately, decorate with swirls of whipped cream and chocolate curls.

FREEZING DETAILS
1. Prepare the recipe to the end of step 5.
2. Cover, seal, label and freeze for up to 3 months.
DEFROSTING DETAILS
Power Setting: Defrost
Defrosting Time: 34 minutes
1. Remove all wrappings. Cook on defrost power for 4 minutes, checking constantly. Leave to stand for 30 minutes.
2. Decorate with swirls of whipped cream and chocolate curls.

CHESTNUT CHARLOTTE RUSSE

Serves 6
150 ml (¼ pint) lemon jelly, made up but not set
5 candied lemon slices, halved
angelica, cut into strips
24 sponge fingers
300 ml (½ pint) milk
2 eggs
1 tablespoon caster sugar
2-3 drops vanilla essence
150 ml (¼ pint) canned sweetened chestnut purée
7 g (¼ oz) powdered gelatine
1 tablespoon water
1 tablespoon lemon juice
300 ml (½ pint) double or whipping cream
To decorate:
whipped cream
marrons glacés

Power Setting: Full/Maximum
Preparation and Cooking Time: 40 minutes, plus chilling

1. Lightly oil the bottom of a 1 litre (1¾ pint) charlotte mould. Pour in a very thin layer of the lemon jelly and chill to set.
2. Place the lemon slices and strips of angelica in a decorative pattern on top of the jelly and pour over the remaining jelly, taking care not to disturb the lemon slices and angelica from their position. Chill to set.

Chestnut charlotte russe;
Chocolate brandy mousse

3. Arrange the sponge fingers around the sides of the charlotte mould, sugared sides outward.
4. Place the milk in a jug and cook for about 3 minutes or until almost boiling. Lightly beat the eggs, sugar and vanilla essence together. Pour the milk on to this mixture, stir well to blend and strain back into the jug.
5. Return to the cooker in a water bath containing hand-hot water and cook for 4 minutes, stirring every 1 minute to keep the sauce smooth. The custard is cooked when it lightly coats the back of the spoon. Allow to cool slightly, then whisk in the chestnut purée until well blended.
6. Dissolve the gelatine in the water and lemon juice. Cook for ½-1 minute until clear and dissolved. Stir into the custard mixture, blending well. Chill until the custard mixture is almost set.
7. Whip the cream until it stands in soft peaks. Fold the cream into the custard mixture and pour into the prepared charlotte mould. Chill until set.
8. To serve, trim the sponge fingers, dip the mould briefly into hot water and invert the charlotte on to a serving dish. Decorate with whipped cream and marrons glacés.

FREEZING DETAILS
1. Prepare the recipe to the end of step 7.
2. Cover the mould with aluminium foil, seal, label and freeze for up to 1 month.
DEFROSTING DETAILS
Power Setting: Defrost
Defrosting Time: 30 minutes
1. Remove all wrappings. Dip the mould briefly into hot water and invert the charlotte on to a serving dish. Cook on defrost power for 5 minutes, checking constantly. Leave to stand for 25 minutes.
2. Decorate with whipped cream and marrons glacés.

GOLDEN HARVEST PEARS WITH CIDER CREAM

4 ripe pears
4 tablespoons golden syrup
grated rind of 1 small lemon
85 ml (3 fl oz) vintage cider
1 tablespoon lemon juice
Cider cream:
150 ml (¼ pint) double or whipping cream
3 tablespoons vintage cider
1 egg
25 g (1 oz) caster sugar
1 teaspoon lemon juice

Power Setting: Full/Maximum
Preparation and Cooking Time: 20 minutes

1. Peel the pears, keeping the stalks intact.
2. Place the syrup in a shallow dish and cook for ½ minute.

3. Stand the pears in the dish and brush each with the hot syrup. Sprinkle with the lemon rind. Cover and cook for 3 minutes.
4. Pour over the cider and lemon juice, brush again with the juices. Cover and cook for 2 minutes. Leave to stand for 5 minutes.
5. To serve immediately, prepare the cider cream. Whip the cream, gradually adding the cider, until thick.
6. Whisk the egg and sugar together until very thick and fluffy. Add the cream mixture and whisk until very thick. Chill lightly.
7. Serve the pears warm or cold with the chilled cider cream.

FREEZING DETAILS
1. Prepare the recipe to the end of step 4.
2. Cool the pears quickly, place in a rigid container with their juices, cover, seal, label and freeze for up to 1 month.
REHEATING DETAILS
Power Setting: Defrost and Full/Maximum
Defrosting and Cooking Time: 15-16 minutes
1. Remove all wrappings. Cover and cook on defrost power for 8 minutes. Leave to stand for 5 minutes.
2. To serve hot, reheat on full/maximum power for 2-3 minutes.
3. Continue from step 5 above to make the cider cream.

TRIO TRUFFLES

Makes 40-45

200 ml (7 fl oz) double cream
vanilla essence
450 g (1 lb) plain chocolate, broken into pieces
40 g (1 ½ oz) butter
½ Jamaica ginger cake
about 50 g (2 oz) chocolate vermicelli
about 50 g (2 oz) long-thread coconut
about 75 g (3 oz) chopped nuts

Power Setting: Full/Maximum
Preparation and Cooking Time: about 20-25 minutes,
plus cooling and chilling

1. Place the cream in a bowl. Cook for 2-3 minutes until hot but not boiling. Stir in a few drops of vanilla essence.
2. Place the chocolate in a bowl and cook for 5-7 minutes to melt, stirring and checking regularly. Blend with the cream.
3. Chill the mixture until beginning to set, then beat in the butter until the mixture is light and fluffy.
4. Rub the ginger cake through a coarse sieve and beat into the cool truffle mixture. Allow the mixture to set a little, then divide into small walnut-sized pieces and roll into small balls.
5. Divide the truffles into 3 portions and roll one portion in chocolate vermicelli, a second in coconut, and the third in nuts.
6. Place in paper sweet cases to serve as an after dinner treat.

FREEZING DETAILS
1. Prepare the recipe to the end of step 5.
2. Place in a rigid box, interleaved with greaseproof paper or freezer film. Cover, seal, label and freeze for up to 6 months.
DEFROSTING DETAILS
Power Setting: Defrost
Defrosting Time: 32-33 minutes
1. Remove all wrappings. Place the truffles in paper cases (not metallic) in a ring on a large plate. Cook on defrost power for 2-3 minutes, checking constantly. Leave to stand for 30 minutes.

Golden harvest pears with cider cream; Trio truffles

COOKING FROM FROZEN

KIPPER AND CORN KEDGEREE

225 g (8 oz) long-grain rice
600 ml (1 pint) boiling water
450 g (1 lb) frozen kipper fillets
50 g (2 oz) butter, diced
175 g (6 oz) frozen sweetcorn kernels
grated rind of 1 lemon
2 tablespoons chopped fresh parsley
salt
freshly ground black pepper
pinch of ground nutmeg
2 tablespoons double cream
To garnish:
1 hard-boiled egg, shelled and quartered
sprigs of fresh parsley

Power Setting: Defrost and Full/Maximum
Preparation and Cooking Time: 40 minutes

1. Place the rice in a deep container with the water. Cover and cook on full/maximum power for 12 minutes. Leave to stand, covered, while preparing the kipper fillets.
2. Place the kipper fillets in a single layer in a large shallow dish and cook them on defrost power for 3 minutes. Allow to stand for 5 minutes.
3. Cook on defrost power for a further 2-3 minutes, until completely thawed.
4. Cover with cling film, snipping 2 holes in the top to allow any steam to escape and cook on full/maximum power for 6 minutes, turning the dish once. Remove, discard any skin and bones and flake into the rice, blending well.
5. Place the butter in a medium bowl and cook on full/maximum power for 1 minute. Add the sweetcorn and lemon rind. Cover and cook on full/maximum power for 3 minutes, stirring once. Stir into the rice with the parsley, salt, pepper and nutmeg to taste.
6. Stir in the double cream, cover and cook on full/maximum power for 1 minute.
7. Serve garnished with hard-boiled egg quarters and parsley.

ONE DISH CHICKEN SUPPER

8 frozen chicken thigh portions
450 g (1 lb) frozen new potatoes
1 tablespoon oil
1 onion, peeled and chopped
100 g (4 oz) frozen button mushrooms
1 × 450 g (1 lb) packet frozen stir-fry vegetables with
*   cauliflower, mushrooms, peas, onions and carrots*
150 ml (¼ pint) apple juice
salt
freshly ground black pepper
To garnish
1 tablespoon chopped fresh parsley

Power Setting: Defrost and Full/Maximum
Preparation and Cooking Time: 55 minutes

1. Place the frozen chicken thigh portions on a plate and cook on defrost power for 12-14 minutes, turning once. Allow to stand while thawing the potatoes.
2. Place the potatoes in a bowl and cook on defrost power for 10 minutes, stirring once.
3. Remove the bone from each chicken thigh portion and cut the meat into slices.
4. Preheat a large browning dish on full/maximum power for 8 minutes (or according to the manufacturer's instructions). Brush with the oil and cook on full/maximum power for a further 2 minutes.
5. Stir in the chicken slices and onion and turn quickly on all sides to brown evenly. Cover and cook on full/maximum power for 6 minutes, stirring once.
6. Add the mushrooms, stir-fry vegetables, potatoes, apple juice and salt and pepper to taste. Cover and cook on full/maximum power for 12 minutes, stirring twice.
7. Serve hot, sprinkled with chopped parsley and accompanied by crusty brown rolls and a mixed salad.

One dish chicken supper;
Kipper and corn kedgeree

SPANISH PAELLA

225 g (8 oz) long-grain rice
600 ml (1 pint) boiling fish stock
1 red pepper, cored, seeded and chopped
½ teaspoon ground turmeric
100 g (4 oz) frozen crab meat
450 g (1 lb) frozen mussels on their half shells
350 g (12 oz) frozen king prawns
100 g (4 oz) cooked chicken, chopped
few drops of anchovy essence
salt
freshly ground black pepper
50 g (2 oz) frozen peas

Power Setting: Full/Maximum and Defrost
Preparation and Cooking Time: 35-40 minutes

1. Place the rice in a deep container with the fish stock, red pepper and turmeric, blending well. Cover and cook on full/maximum power for 12 minutes. Leave to stand, covered.
2. Meanwhile place the crab meat in a bowl and cook on defrost power for 5 minutes.
3. Shell all but 4 of the prawns. Place the mussels and all the prawns in a bowl and cook on defrost power for 9-11 minutes, stirring every 2 minutes until thawed. Reserve the 4 prawns.
4. Flake the crab meat into the rice. Add the remaining ingredients. Cover and cook on full/maximum power for 4-6 minutes, stirring once. Garnish with the reserved prawns.

MEXICAN SAUSAGES

450 g (1 lb) frozen pork sausages, hot spicy variety if available
100 g (4 oz) frozen sweetcorn kernels
1 tablespoon oil
1 onion, peeled and chopped
1 small red pepper, cored, seeded and chopped
½ teaspoon mustard powder
½-1 teaspoon chilli powder
salt
freshly ground black pepper
2 sticks frozen double cream (the equivalent of 3 tablespoons)

Power Setting: Defrost and Full/Maximum
Preparation and Cooking Time: 35 minutes

1. Cook the sausages on a plate on defrost power for 5 minutes, turning them once. Leave to stand for 5 minutes. Prick with a fork.
2. Cook the sweetcorn in a bowl on defrost power for 2 minutes.
3. Preheat a lidded browning dish on full/maximum power for 8 minutes (or according to the manufacturer's instructions). Brush with the oil and cook on full/maximum power for a further 2 minutes. Add the sausages and turn quickly on all sides to brown.
4. Combine all ingredients except cream. Cover and cook on full/maximum power for 10 minutes, stirring twice. Add the cream and cook on full power for 2 minutes, stirring once.

CHICKEN LIVER RISOTTO

450 g (1 lb) frozen chicken livers
1 tablespoon oil
1 large onion, peeled and chopped
2 × 275 g (10 oz) packets frozen vegetable rice with
*   sweetcorn and peppers*
200 ml (7 fl oz) dry cider
200 ml (7 fl oz) water
25 g (1 oz) butter
salt
freshly ground black pepper
To garnish:
pepper rings
sprig of fresh parsley

Power Setting: Defrost and Full/Maximum
Preparation and Cooking Time: 45 minutes

1. Place the chicken livers in a bowl and cook on defrost power for 9 minutes until completely thawed. Rinse and cut into pieces.
2. Place the oil and onion in a large bowl and cook on full/maximum power for 4 minutes, stirring once.
3. Stir in the vegetable rice, cider, water, butter and salt and pepper. Cover and cook on full/maximum power for 20 minutes, stirring twice during the cooking time. Leave to stand for 5 minutes.
4. Garnish with pepper rings a and parsley. Serve hot with crusty sesame bread and a green salad.

PEPPERED MACKEREL PÂTÉ

350 g (12 oz) frozen peppered smoked mackerel fillets
75 g (3 oz) butter
2 tablespoon lemon juice
pinch of ground nutmeg
To garnish:
lemon slices

Power Setting: Full/Maximum
Preparation and Cooking Time: 10 minutes

1. Place the mackerel fillets in a bowl. Cover and cook for 3½ minutes. Leave to stand, covered, for 5 minutes.
2. Flake the mackerel into a blender goblet, removing and discarding any skin and bones. Add the butter, lemon juice and nutmeg. Purée until smooth and creamy.
3. Spoon into 4 small ramekins or dishes.
4. Garnish with the lemon slices and serve lightly chilled with hot toast fingers or crisp crackers.

CLOCKWISE FROM TOP LEFT: Spanish paella;
Chicken liver risotto; Mexican sausages

ORIENTAL CHICKEN WITH SWEET AND SOUR SAUCE

4 × 255 g (9 oz) frozen chicken portions
1 tablespoon oil
1 onion, peeled and thinly sliced
1 small green pepper, cored, seeded and sliced
1 small red pepper, cored, seeded and sliced
1 garlic clove, peeled and chopped
pinch of ground ginger
salt
freshly ground black pepper
1½ tablespoons red wine vinegar
1 tablespoon brown sugar
150 ml (¼ pint) apple juice
150 ml (¼ pint) unsweetened orange juice
1 tablespoon cornflour
1 small carrot, peeled and coarsely grated
2 canned pineapple rings, coarsely chopped
25 g (1 oz) pine nuts

To garnish:
spring onion tassel

Power Setting: Defrost and Full/Maximum
Preparation and Cooking Time: 1 hour 15 minutes

1. Place the frozen chicken portions on a microwave roasting rack and cook on defrost power for 14 minutes.
2. Cook on full/maximum power for 20 minutes, turning and re-arranging the chicken every 5 minutes.
3. Place the oil, onion, peppers and garlic in a casserole. Cover and cook on full/maximum power for 6 minutes, stirring once. Add the ginger, salt and pepper, vinegar, sugar, apple and orange juice. Cover and cook on full/maximum power for 4 minutes.
4. Blend the cornflour with a little water and stir into the sauce with the carrot and pineapple pieces, blending well. Cover and cook for 3 minutes, stirring once.
5. Add the chicken pieces and nuts. Cover and cook on full/maximum power for 4 minutes. Allow to stand for 5 minutes. Garnish with a spring onion tassel.

HADDOCK MORNAY SHELLS

2 × 198 g (7 oz) packets frozen buttered smoked haddock
25 g (1 oz) butter
25 g (1 oz) plain flour
300 ml (½ pint) milk
1 egg yolk, beaten
1 teaspoon made mustard
salt
freshly ground black pepper
75 g (3 oz) Cheddar cheese, grated
2 teaspoons chopped capers

Power Setting: Full/Maximum
Preparation and Cooking Time: 25 minutes

1. Pierce each packet of haddock and place on a plate. Cook on full/maximum power for 10 minutes, shaking the packets gently after 6 minutes. Leave to stand while preparing the sauce.
2. Place the butter in a jug and cook on full/maximum power for ½ minute to melt. Add the flour, mixing well. Gradually add the milk and cook on full/maximum power for 3½-4 minutes, stirring every 1 minute until the sauce is smooth and thickened. Beat in the egg yolk, mustard, salt and pepper to taste and half the cheese.
3. Flake the haddock, discarding any skin. Fold into the sauce with the capers. Spoon into 4 scallop shells or flameproof dishes. Sprinkle with the remaining cheese and cook on full/maximum power for 2 minutes, re-arranging the dishes after 1 minute.
4. Brown quickly under a preheated hot grill.
5. Serve with triangles of hot toast.

LIGHT SUMMER CURRY

750 g (1½ lb) frozen firm white fish fillets (e.g. cod, rock`
  salmon)
1 onion, peeled and chopped
25 g (1 oz) butter
25 g (1 oz) plain flour
2 teaspoons hot Madras curry powder
200 ml (7 fl oz) water
1½ tablespoons lemon juice
2 firm tomatoes, peeled, seeded and chopped
6 sticks frozen double cream (equivalent to 150 ml (¼ pint)
salt

Power Setting: Defrost and Full/Maximum
Preparation and Cooking Time: 30 minutes

1. Place the fish fillets in a dish and cook on defrost power for 12 minutes. Leave to stand while preparing the sauce.
2. Place the onion and butter in a bowl. Cover and cook on full power for 2 minutes, stirring once. Stir in the flour and curry powder, blending well. Gradually add the water and lemon juice. Cover and cook on full/maximum power for 2½ minutes, stirring every 1 minute.
3. Meanwhile, skin the fish fillets and place in a serving dish. Pour over the sauce. Cover and cook on full/maximum power for 5 minutes, stirring or re-arranging the fish fillets twice.
4. Carefully add the tomatoes and frozen cream sticks with salt to taste. Cover and cook on full/maximum power for 4 minutes, stirring twice. Serve with boiled rice.

Oriental chicken with sweet and sour sauce; Haddock mornay shells

PLAICE BONNE FEMME

4 frozen plaice fillets
50 g (2 oz) butter
25 g (1 oz) plain flour
150 ml (¼ pint) milk
150 ml (¼ pint) dry white wine
2 small onions, peeled and chopped
100 g (4 oz) button mushrooms, chopped
1 tablespoon lemon juice
salt
freshly ground white pepper
To garnish:
sprigs of fresh parsley

Power Setting: Defrost and Full/Maximum
Preparation and Cooking Time: 35 minutes

1. Place the fish fillets in a dish and cook on defrost power for 7-8 minutes. Leave to stand while preparing the sauce.
2. Place half the butter in a jug and cook on full/maximum power for ½ minute to melt. Add the flour, blending well. Gradually add the milk and wine and cook on full/maximum power for 3½-4 minutes, stirring every 1 minute until smooth and thickened.
3. Place half of the remaining butter in a bowl with the onion and mushrooms. Cover and cook on full/maximum power for 4 minutes, stirring once. Stir into the sauce.
4. Skin the thawed fish fillets. Sprinkle with the lemon juice and salt and pepper to taste. Roll up from the tail end and place in a serving dish. Dot with the remaining butter. Cover and cook on full/maximum power for 5-7 minutes, turning once.
5. Strain any fish cooking juices fish into the sauce. Spoon over the fish, cover and cook for 2 minutes. Garnish with parsley.

POTTED SHRIMPS

350 g (12 oz) frozen peeled shrimps or prawns
175 g (6 oz) butter, diced
salt
pinch of ground mace
pinch of cayenne pepper
To garnish:
sprigs of fresh parsley
lemon wedges

Power Setting: Defrost and Full/Maximum
Preparation and Cooking Time: 10 minutes

1. Place the frozen shrimps or prawns in a bowl and cook on defrost power for 6-7 minutes, stirring once. Drain and discard any thaw juices.
2. Place the butter in a bowl and cook on full/maximum power for 1½ minutes, stirring once, to melt. Add the shrimps or prawns, salt, mace and cayenne pepper to taste. Divide equally between 4 small ramekin dishes.
3. Garnish with parsley and lemon wedges.

SAUSAGE AND HORSERADISH ROLY-POLY

Serves 6
Suet Pastry:
225 g (8 oz) self-raising flour
pinch of salt
100 g (4 oz) shredded suet
150 ml (¼ pint) cold water
Filling:
450 g (1 lb) frozen beef sausages
15 g (½ oz) butter
100g (4 oz) mushrooms, wiped and sliced
2 teaspoons creamed horseradish
salt
freshly ground black pepper
provençal sauce (see Pork spareribs provençal, page 33)
To garnish:
sprig of fresh parsley

Power Setting: Defrost and Full/Maximum
Preparation and Cooking Time: about 30 minutes

1. Place the sausages on a plate and cook on defrost power for 5 minutes, turning and re-arranging them once. Leave to stand while preparing the mushrooms.
2. Place the butter and mushrooms in a bowl, cook on full/maximum power for 2 minutes, stirring once. Stir in the creamed horseradish and salt and pepper to taste.
3. Prick the sausages well with a fork. Cook on full/maximum power for 4-4½ minutes, turning and re-arranging them once. Cut into thin slices.
4. Mix the sausages with the mushroom mixture, blending well.
5. Sift the flour and salt into a bowl. Stir in the suet. Add the cold water and mix to a soft but manageable dough. Roll out the dough on a lightly floured surface to a 23 cm (9 inch) square.
6. Spread the sausage mixture evenly over the suet pastry square, leaving a 1 cm (½ inch) border around the edge, and carefully roll up like a Swiss roll.
7. Place, seam side down, on a piece of greaseproof paper and roll the greaseproof up loosely around the pastry roll, allowing plenty of space for the roly-poly to rise. Carefully tie the ends of the paper with string or elastic bands and cover loosely with cling film.
8. Cook for 8 minutes, turning twice, until well risen and cooked through. Test by inserting a skewer into the centre of the roll – the skewer should come out clean and free from dough.
9. Serve hot immediately, cut into slices, with the provençal sauce. Garnish with parsley.

Suet pastry can be made lighter by adding 50 g (2 oz) fresh white breadcrumbs with the suet. Bind together with a little extra water if necessary. Ring the changes and flavour with ½ small grated onion or 1-2 teaspoons chopped fresh herbs.

FROM THE LEFT: Potted shrimps; Turkey roast with prune and mustard sauce; Sausage and horseradish roly-poly

TURKEY ROAST WITH PRUNE AND MUSTARD SAUCE

1 × 600 g (1 ¼ lb) frozen boneless turkey breast roast
25 g (1 oz) butter
2 teaspoons mustard powder
salt
freshly ground black pepper
150 ml (¼ pint) port
175 g (6 oz) stoneless prunes
2 teaspoons cornflour
150 ml (¼ pint) chicken stock
To garnish:
sprigs of watercress

Power Setting: Defrost and Full/Maximum
Preparation and Cooking Time: 45 minutes

1. Place the turkey roast in a lidded dish and cook on defrost power for 8 minutes. Allow to stand for 5-10 minutes until completely thawed.
2. Spread with the butter and rub with the mustard powder and salt and pepper to taste. Cover and cook on full/maximum power for 6 minutes.
3. Turn the turkey roast over, baste with the juices, cover and cook on full/maximum power for a further 5-6 minutes. Remove from the dish, wrap in aluminium foil and leave to stand while preparing the sauce.
4. Add the port and prunes to the dish juices. Cover and cook on full/maximum power for 4 minutes.
5. Mix the cornflour with the stock and stir into the prune and port mixture. Cover and cook on full/maximum power for 4 minutes, stirring twice.
6. Carve the turkey roast into slices and garnish with the prunes and watercress. Pour over a little of the sauce and serve the rest separately.

EASY SPEEDY MOUSSAKA

450 g (1 lb) aubergines, trimmed and finely sliced
salt
2 × 200 g (7 oz) packets frozen lamb grillsteaks
1 × 200 g (7 oz) can tomatoes
2 teaspoons dried oregano or basil
freshly ground black pepper
3 tablespoons oil
2 eggs, beaten
300 ml (½ pint) plain unsweetened yogurt
100 g (4 oz) Cheddar cheese, grated

To garnish:
tomato wedges
sprigs of fresh parlsey

Power Setting: Full/Maximum and Defrost
Preparation and Cooking Time: 1 hour 15 minutes

1. Sprinkle the aubergine slices with salt and leave to stand and drain for 30 minutes.

Savoury vegetable flan; Easy speedy moussaka;
Salmon trout with hollandaise sauce

2. Meanwhile, place the frozen lamb grillsteaks in a shallow dish. Cook on full/maximum power for 7 minutes, rearranging and turning the grillsteaks once.

3. Mix the tomatoes and their juice with the oregano or basil, salt and pepper. Cover and cook on full/maximum power for 2 minutes.

4. Place the oil in a large dish and cook on full/maximum power for 1 minute. Rinse and dry the aubergine slices. Add to the oil and toss well to coat. Cover and cook on full/maximum power for 8-10 minutes until tender, shaking the dish twice.

5. Line the base of a serving dish with half of the aubergine slices. Top with the cooked lamb grillsteaks. Spoon over the tomato mixture and top with the remaining aubergine slices.

6. Cover and cook on full/maximum power for 3 minutes, turning the dish once.

7. Beat the eggs with the yogurt and stir in three-quarters of the cheese. Pour over the aubergines and cook on defrost power for 9-10 minutes or until the topping is set.

8. Sprinkle with the remaining cheese and grill until golden and bubbly. Garnish with tomato wedges and parsley sprigs.

SAVOURY VEGETABLE FLAN

1 × 225 g (8 oz) packet frozen shortcrust pastry
1 × 140 g (5 oz) packet frozen mixed vegetables
25 g (1 oz) butter
1 small onion, peeled and chopped
75 ml (2½ fl oz) milk
2 eggs, beaten
salt
freshly ground black pepper
1 tablespoon chopped fresh parsley
75 g (3 oz) cheese, grated

Power Setting: Defrost and Full/Maximum
Preparation and Cooking Time: 1 hour

1. Place the pastry on a plate and cook on defrost power for 1 minute. Leave to stand for 15 minutes.
2. Meanwhile, place the vegetables in a bowl and cook on defrost power for 4 minutes.
3. Place the butter in a bowl and cook on full/maximum power for ½ minute. Add the onion, cover and cook on full/maximum power for 3 minutes.
4. Mix the vegetables with the onion, milk, eggs, salt and pepper to taste, parsley and half the cheese.
5. Roll out the pastry on a lightly floured surface to a round large enough to line a 20 cm (8 inch) flan dish. Press in firmly, taking care not to stretch the pastry. Cut the pastry away, leaving a 5 mm (¼ inch) 'collar' above the dish to allow for any shrinkage that may occur (page 37). Prick the base and sides well with a fork. Place a double thickness layer of paper towel above the base, easing into position around the edges.
6. Cook on full/maximum power for 3½ minutes, giving the dish a quarter turn every 1 minute. Remove the paper and cook on full/maximum power for a further 1½ minutes.
7. Spoon the filling into the flan case and sprinkle with the remaining cheese. Cook on defrost power for 14-16 minutes, giving the dish a quarter-turn every 3 minutes. Allow to stand for 10-15 minutes. The flan should set completely during this standing time.

Variation:

Savoury Coriander, Mushroom and Vegetable Flan: Prepare and cook as above but add 50 g (2 oz) chopped cooked button mushrooms to the vegetables and 1 tablespoon chopped fresh coriander instead of the parsley. For an extra special flavour, try using a flavoured Cheddar cheese (e.g. Cheddar with chives, Cheddar with pickle or Cheddar with mustard).

SALMON TROUT WITH HOLLANDAISE SAUCE

Serves 8
1 × 1.75 kg (4 lb) frozen salmon trout, cleaned
2 tablespoons lemon juice
4 tablespoons boiling water
Hollandaise sauce:
225 g (8 oz) butter
6 tablespoons lemon juice
1 teaspoon mustard powder
4 egg yolks
salt
freshly ground white pepper
To garnish:
lemon wedges
cucumber slices

Power Setting: Defrost and Full/Maximum
Preparation and Cooking Time: 1 hour 20 minutues

1. Place the salmon trout in a shallow dish (curled round if necessary) and cook on defrost power for 20-22 minutes.
2. Drain away any thaw juices. Pour over the lemon juice and boiling water. Prick the salmon skin in several places to prevent it from bursting during cooking. Shield the tail end and head (if present) with small pieces of aluminium foil (see note on shielding, page 6). Cover and cook on full/maximum power for 28 minutes, giving the dish a turn every 7 minutes. Allow to cool slightly, then remove the skin.
3. Prepare the sauce by placing the butter in a large jug. Cook on full/maximum power for 2 minutes. Mix the lemon juice with the mustard and egg yolks and whisk into the hot butter. Whisk well to blend smoothly, then add salt and pepper to taste.
4. Cook on medium power for 1½ minutes, taking care to ensure that the sauce does not boil. Serve hot with the salmon. Garnish with lemon wedges and cucumber slices.

Prick the salmon in several places to prevent it bursting during cooking.

Shield the tail end and head (if present) with small pieces of aluminium foil.

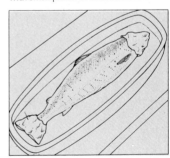

GOOSEBERRY AND ORANGE CHIFFON

175 g (6 oz) frozen gooseberries
50 g (2 oz) sugar
100 ml (3½ fl oz) water
1 × 135 g (4¾ oz) packet orange table jelly
300 ml (½ pint) double cream
green or orange liquid food colouring (optional)
16 sponge fingers or langue de chat biscuits

Power Setting: Defrost and Full/Maximum
Preparation and Cooking Time: 20 minutes, plus cooling and chilling

1. Place the gooseberries in a bowl and cook on defrost power for 4 minutes, stirring once. Add the sugar, mixing well. Cover and cook on full/maximum power for 2 minutes. Purée in a blender or pass through a fine sieve.
2. Place the water and jelly tablet in a jug and cook on full power for 2-3 minutes or until the jelly has dissolved. Stir in the gooseberry purée and make up to 450 ml (¾ pint) with water. Allow to cool until almost set.
3. Whip the cream until it stands in soft peaks. Whisk the setting jelly mixture until foamy, then whisk in the cream. Colour light green or orange with food colouring if wished. Turn into a 675 g (1½ lb) loaf dish.
4. Chill for about ½-1 hour until set. To serve, dip the loaf dish briefly into hot water and turn out on to a serving dish. Decorate the sides with sponge fingers or langue de chat biscuits.

BLACKCURRANT SORBET

1 kg (2 lb) frozen blackcurrants
4 tablespoons clear honey
225 g (8 oz) sugar
300 ml (½ pint) water
2 egg whites
To garnish:
sprigs of mint

Power Setting: Defrost and Full/Maximum
Preparation and Cooking Time: 20 minutes, plus
freezing

1. Place the blackcurrants in a bowl. Cover and cook on defrost power for 6 minutes, stirring twice.
2. Add the honey, sugar and water, blending well. Cover and cook on full/maximum power for 6-8 minutes until the blackcurrants are cooked, stirring once.
3. Purée in a blender or rub through a fine sieve. Place in a freezer tray and freeze for about 2 hours until half frozen.
4. Whisk the egg whites until they stand in stiff peaks. Whisk the half-frozen purée until slushy. Fold in the egg whites, return to the freezer and freeze until firm.
5. Serve scooped into glasses. Garnish with mint.

FLORIDA ORANGE SOUFFLÉ

1 × 175 ml (6 fl oz) can orange juice concentrate
3 eggs, separated
75 g (3 oz) caster sugar
1 tablespoon Cointreau
1 tablespoon lemon juice
15 g (½ oz) powdered gelatine
3 tablespoons water
150 ml (¼ pint) double cream
To decorate:
chopped nuts
whipped cream
crystallized orange slices

Power Setting: Defrost and Full/Maximum
Preparation and Cooking Time: 30 minutes, plus
chilling

1. Remove the metal lid (if present) from the can of orange concentrate and cook on defrost power for 2-3 minutes stirring twice. Leave to stand for 5 minutes.

RASPBERRY YOGURT ICE CREAM

225 g (8 oz) frozen raspberries
2 eggs, beaten
450 ml (¾ pint) milk
175 g (6 oz) sugar
150 ml (¼ pint) double cream
150 ml (¼ pint) plain unsweetened yogurt

Power Setting: Defrost and Full/Maximum
Preparation and Cooking Time: 20 minutes, plus
cooling and freezing

1. Place the raspberries in a bowl and cook on defrost power for 4 minutes. Purée three-quarters of the raspberries in a blender or pass through a fine sieve.
2. Mix the eggs, milk and sugar in a bowl and cook on full/maximum power for 6 minutes, stirring every 2 minutes. Allow to cool.
3. Stir in the cream, yogurt and raspberry purée, blending well. Pour into a freezer tray and freeze until almost solid.
4. Remove from the freezer and whisk until smooth. Fold in the whole raspberries and return to the freezer. Freeze until firm.
5. Serve scooped into glasses.

2. Lightly grease a 600 ml (1 pint) soufflé dish. Cut a double strip of greaseproof paper, equal in width to the height of the dish plus 5 cm (2 inches) and long enough to go right round the outside of the dish. Lightly grease the top 5 cm (2 inches) and tie securely with string around the outside of the dish, greased side inward.
3. Beat the egg yolks with the sugar until thick and creamy. Whisk in half of the orange concentrate (use the remainder for another dish or for drinks), Cointreau and lemon juice.
4. Mix the gelatine with the water in a small bowl and leave until the water has been absorbed. Cook on full/maximum power for ½ minute until clear and dissolved. Allow to cool slightly.
5. Whisk the egg whites until they stand in soft peaks and whip the cream until stiff. Stir the gelatine into the orange mixture, then fold in the cream and finally the egg whites. Pour gently into the prepared soufflé dish.
6. Chill for about 2-4 hours until set.
7. To serve, carefully ease the greaseproof paper away from the soufflé, using the back of a knife. Press chopped nuts around the sides of the soufflé. Decorate the top with swirls of whipped cream and crystallized orange slices.

Gooseberry and orange chiffon;
Blackcurrant sorbet;
Florida orange soufflé

INDEX